SEX INTERVIEWS SIMPLIFIED

A Guide to Victim Interviewing and Suspect Confessions

Don Howell

LawTech Publishing

SEX CRIME INTERVIEWS SIMPLIFIED - Copyright©1999-2009 Don Howell
[All rights reserved. This publication is protected by Copyright and permission should be obtained from the publisher prior to any prohibited reproduction, storage in a retrieval system, or transmission in any form or by any means, electronic, mechanical, photocopying, recording, or likewise. For information regarding permission(s), contact Rights and Permissions Department.]

This book is a compilation of Don's two previous titles:
A Guide To Interviewing Sex Crime Victims
(ISBN 13: 978-1-930466-29-6 & ISBN 10: 1-9930466-29-3)
and
Interviewing Sexually Motivated Offenders
(ISBN: 1-56325-098-5)

Published by:
LawTech Publishing Co.
Phone: 1(800)498.0911
Fax: 1(949)498.4858
info@lawtechpublishing.com
www.lawtechpublishing.com

LawTech is a division of *LawTech Group*, www.lawtechgroup.com.

v.05.04.09

pp. 196

Disclaimer:

The information in this book is not intended to be used as the only resource to develop probable cause to make an arrest. Nor is it evidence, in and of itself, to prosecute someone in court. It is based on the author's personal experiences as a sex crimes investigator and is only intended to be used as an investigative guide.

Always check with your own department and local prosecutor's policies before implementing any action based on information in this book. The information herein is not intended to supersede any local, state or federal statutes and/or case law.

Printed in the United States of America.

ISBN: 978-1-56325-144-3

About the Author

Don was 15-years old when he knew he wanted to be a police detective. By age 21, he had graduated with honors from the California State University at Los Angeles with a Bachelor of Science Degree in Police Science and Administration. For the next 35 years he "studied" in the "university of law enforcement." Twenty-seven of those years as a detective investigating sexually motivated crimes.

Don is a 25 year member of the California Sexual Assault Investigators Association and, in 2002, was awarded their Sustained Achievement Award for his years in service.

Don retired from full time police work after 30 years, but was rehired the same day as a part time detective, where he currently investigates sex crimes and cold case homicides.

Don also lectures at the Delinquency Control Institute (DCI) on the campus of the University of Southern California (USC) and has guest lectured at many colleges, universities and conferences.

Acknowledgments

There are many people who have contributed directly and indirectly to the writing of this book. On the victim side of the equation is Marie and hundreds of others who shared with me their personal experiences, thoughts, feelings and courage to come forward and move forward with their lives. They've taught me more than any book ever could.

On the suspect side it was FBI agent Bob Morneau who first peaked my interest in sex offenders in 1973, when he lectured at the police academy. He forced me to expand my thinking about sexually motivated crimes and to set aside my own ideas about what is normal and develop a forensic mind set.

The outstanding work of Dr. Nicholas Groth in the area of rapists and child molesters laid a foundation for me and many others to add a behavioral component to my investigations. FBI agents Roy Hazelwood and Ken Lanning were also instrumental in expanding my understanding of sex offenders. These are just a few of the lecturers and investigators I've been fortunate enough to encounter over the years.

To the Huntington Beach Police Department for allowing me to stay at my detective desk for almost three decades, working case after case, interviewing thousands of victims and suspects; testing the theories and developing the contents of this book.

Special thanks to Susan Davidson, a long time friend, co-author and founder of the California branch of the National Center for Missing and Exploited Children (originally know as the Adam Walsh Resource Center). Susan is a true visionary who saw a problem with kidnapped and sexually victimized children and moved toward a solution. She knew the only way to reduce the sexual victimization of children was to educate an entire country and develop new and stronger laws to reduce repeat offenders. She's still working towards that goal.

I would also like to thank my son Paul for his help with the graphics, Doreen Weaver for her typing and organizational skills along with Judy Smith whose editing talents made this book possible.

Lastly, I'd like to express my appreciation and love for my sons, Eric and Paul for putting up with me, the long hours, the late night call-outs and missed weekends. And to my daughter Sophie, who proved to me it was all worth it.

TABLE OF CONTENTS

INTRODUCTION 1

Part I: Interviewing Sex Crime Victims

1. **GET IT RIGHT! GET IT ALL! GET IT THE FIRST TIME!** 5
   Interview Reports - Confidentiality 6
2. **INTERVIEWING CHILDREN AGES 2-7** 8
   Background Information 9
   First Contact with the Child Using The Stick Figure System (SFS) 10
   Physical Setting For The Interview 10
   Rapport Building 12
   Identifying Body Parts 13
   Pre-Drawn Anatomy 16
   Use of Anatomically Correct Dolls 20
   Good Touch vs. Bad Touch 20
   Qualifying as a Witness 20
   Attention Span 21
   Number of Counts 22
   Time Frames 22
   Secrets 22
   Other Victims 23
   Doing it Correctly 23
   Interview of Child 2-7 Years Using The Stick Figure System 23
   False Reports 31
   Repeating Questions 32
   Tape-recording / Videotaping 32
   Teaming With Social Services 34
   Protective Custody 34
   ASAV: Alleged Sexual Assault Victim Examination 36
   Interviews at School 38
   Cross-reporting to the Child Abuse Registry 38
   Photographs as Evidence 39
   INTERVIEW CHECKLIST 42
3. **INTERVIEWING CHILDREN AGES 8-12** 43
   Background 43
   Seating Arrangement 43
   Terminology 43
   Teaming With Social Services 44
   Out-of-Home Suspect 44
   Victim / Suspect Profile 44

TABLE OF CONTENTS

    Victim Gender 45
    Family Dynamics 45
    Number of Counts 45
    Attention Span 46
    Qualifying as a Witness 46
    Discussion 46
    Cross-Reporting 47
    Number of Counts 47
    False Reports 48
    Interview: 8-12 Year-Old Victim 48

4. INTERVIEWING AGES 13-18 . . . . **53**
    Background Information 53
    First Contact with the Victim 53
    Building Rapport with a Teen 54
    Manipulation by Victims 54
    Male Perpetrator - Male Victim 57
    Male Perpetrator - Female Victim 59
    Incest 59
    Female Perpetrators - Female Victims 65
    Female Perpetrators - Male Victims 65
    Example: Adult Female Perpetrator Adolescent Male Victim 67
    Clandestine Telephone Calls from Victims 69
    Date Rape 69
    Sex of Interviewer 70
    Stranger Rape 70
    Medical Exams 70
    False Reports 70

5. INTERVIEWING AGES 18-80 . . . . **72**
    When The Suspect Is A Stranger 72
    Interview: Rape Victim 79
    Date Rape / Acquaintance Rape 92
    Spousal Rape 96
    Senile / Elderly Victims 100
    Mentally Handicapped / Retarded Victims 104
    Satanic Cults 107
    Unlawful Intercourse 110
    To Tape or Not to Tape 112
    When The Victim Won't Talk 113
    Female Anatomy 114
    Teaming Officers and Advocates 115

6. GETTING IT ALL **117**

TABLE OF CONTENTS

Part II: Interviewing Sexually Motivated Offenders

- 7. CASE SELECTION......119
  - Did you ever wonder?......119
- 8. THEY DON'T LIKE EACH OTHER......121
- 9. THE FIVE TRADEMARKS OF A SUSPECT INTERVIEW......132
  - #1 - Diminish the Severity......133
  - #2 - Blame the Victim......134
  - #3 - Control the Interview......136
  - #4 - Never Tell 100 %......137
  - #5 - Never Tell You About Crimes That You Don't Already Know About......139
- 10. ANTI-LOGIC......143
- 11. RAPE FANTASY......145
- 12. THEY DON'T GET IT......146
- 13. SOMETHING'S NOT RIGHT......149
- 14. HOW DID THEY BECOME SEX OFFENDERS?......156
- 15. PUTTING IT ALL TOGETHER......159

APPENDIX A. RAPE TRAUMA SYNDROME......179

APPENDIX B. INDICATORS OF FALSE ALLEGATIONS OF SEXUAL ASSAULT BY STRANGERS......182

BIBLIOGRAPHY......185

INDEX......188

INTRODUCTION

The first section of this text introduces a unique approach to the art of interviewing sex crime victims of all ages. For too long, there has been a void of information, or a "how to" manual on how to talk to this victim group. There are countless materials about the impact of this type of assault and endless lists of behavioral traits of the offenders, but little about how to actually do it, or what to say and ask. This book intends to "cut to the bottom line" and give police, social workers or legal advocates the tools to do the initial interview which will result in:

(a) The comfort of the victim

(b) Getting all the information the first time

(c) The steps to take cases to prosecution

The instructions and examples in this book will give even the novice an "A B C" or "by the numbers" approach to interviewing children. Following these steps will get you started and take you through to the end. It will tell you what to do at the very first contact with the child, where to sit, what to say, and how to close the interview.

The Stick Figure System (SFS) is a method designed for very young children. It provides a framework to work within, which enables the interviewer and the child to have a conversation about the alleged molestation, instead of an awkward question and answer session. By creating simple drawings together, the investigator and the child can build rapport and establish the elements of the crime. These steps vary with the age of the child, but are vital to every case.

When dealing with older children and adults, the steps change. But, it's still easier than you think once you have the basic concepts described in this book. By following these simple techniques, and adding some of your own personality and creativity, you will have all the tools you need for successfully interviewing all type of sex crime victims.

It's impossible to cite the laws of each state as they relate to the investigation and prosecution of sexual abuse. Although we have included examples of California statutes and regulations throughout the text, the reader should carefully research their appropriate state laws and case decisions.

There will always be an offender out there who will do something so totally bizarre it defies any logic or preconceived idea as to what sex offenders normally do. In sex crimes, almost every situation has some new twist or turn. The saying "just when you think you've heard it all," is especially true for sex crimes.

My intent is to raise the level, bar, quality of child interviews, regardless of who is doing them. I'm also a firm believer in "if something is working for you, then keep doing it." So if you currently have a system, style or check list that's working for you, may all means keep using it. If you don't have a system, try mine or at least add some of my ideas to what you are already doing.

The second section of the book jumps the reader into the world of the sex offender and how to use his/her behaviors against him during interview. Over the years, I've gained a great deal of information about sexually motivated crimes. There's a tremendous amount of information available about sex offenders and the types of crimes they commit. For many years, I've tried to figure out a way to use all this information in my daily caseload.

I finally realized the key was to take a step back from the flood of available information about sex offenders. Since no two sex offenders act exactly alike, trying to apply the exact same formula to each of them is difficult. There are many defining characteristics for the different types of sex offenders. However, as you go down the list of behaviors for one type you'll find there is a cross over or blending of traits between one offender type and the next.

The actions of the suspect during a sexual assault should fit together like the pieces of a puzzle. Taking a step back allows you to look at the behavior in a more generalized way. Once you have done this you can ask yourself some questions, such as, "Does the victim's behavior during the crime make sense?" and "Has the victim convinced you that he/she has been in the presence of a sex offender?" "Do you have the six phases of a sexual assault?" If the suspect talks to you, "Are you seeing the five trademarks true sex offenders will exhibit during interview?" When the pieces fit together, you will know which cases are factual and which are not.

INTRODUCTION

I want to emphasize that I am not a profiler. I have the highest regard for those people who have the psychology backgrounds to be able to call themselves such. Whenever possible, I try to "pick the brains" of these people and I suggest you do the same.

The purpose of this book is to lay a foundation for the "routine cases" which make up the vast majority of the sex crimes investigated by law enforcement. These are the cases that pile up on your desk each day. The ones you try to prioritize and decide which ones you're going to work today and which ones you're going to put on hold. This book is intended to give you another tool to help you make those decisions.

I will start by telling you a secret most sex crimes investigators are afraid to mention above a whisper. The secret is, a large percentage of reported offenses do not rise to the level of a prosecutable crime. In fact, many barley have corpus and waste a lot of law enforcement's time, which would be better spent on the more legitimate sex offenses.

This book will help UN-blur the line between legitimate sex crimes and those that will never rise to the level of a criminal prosecution.

For ease of reading, I often use the male gender when referring to suspects and the female gender when referring to victims. Be assured there are female offenders and male victims. The techniques in this book are designed with all sex offenders in mind. From window peepers and indecent exposure to rape and child molesters, the information in this book applies to all of them.

PART I:

INTERVIEWING SEX CRIME VICTIMS

Chapter 1

GET IT RIGHT! GET IT ALL! GET IT THE FIRST TIME!

This text is designed to help you do the above three critical things. It is specifically designed for interviewing sexual assault victims, primarily children. Having been a police officer for over twenty-five years, I know that most officers would rather be involved in a shooting with a band of bank robbers as opposed to interviewing a five year-old who has been fondled by a neighbor. This fear of interviewing children is due to a lack of a plan, or method, about what to actually ask and how to go about asking it. In reality, the younger the child is, the easier it is to interview them, because children of this age have no prejudices, predilections, or preconceived ideas about the actual events which took place. All you need is basic knowledge about how children think, then how to establish a connection between you and the child so that he or she will tell you what you need to know. With a few, simple techniques and procedures, you will be able to *get it right, get it all, and get it the first time.*

While this handbook is written from a law enforcement point of view, the technique, system and principles can be used by social workers, therapists, teachers, lawyers or anyone who needs to obtain factual information from a child and prepare a report as well.

As children get older they become more verbal, which obviously makes communicating with them somewhat easier, but the dynamics of the molestation itself becomes more complex. Fortunately, with a little background as to how and why these crimes occur, you will know what to look for and what questions to ask.

Teenagers and adults present a different set of problems for the interviewer. However, these can also be easily overcome once you have an idea of what to expect and how to present yourself to the victim.

This text will focus mainly on talking to people who have been the victims of some type of sex crime. However, the same principles can apply to victims who have been physically abused, neglected, emotionally abused, and/or have been witnesses to non-sexual crimes, such as robbery, assault, spousal abuse or any other type of criminal activity.

This book is designed to give the novice a starting point as to how to begin the conversation with a sexual assault victim and will also help experienced interviewers fine tune their skills. If you already have some sort of a technique or a style that you use when interviewing children and other victims which is successful for you, by all means continue to use it. Please feel free to add any of this information to the techniques you are already using.

In my experience, I have found that using the methods described here will get you the information needed in about 95% of the cases you encounter.

Sex offenders vary widely in their motivations, psychological dynamics, the fantasies they create for themselves, and in the way they approach and assault both children and adults. This book is not intended to try to describe the various types of sex offenders, but rather is designed to assist you in the *most likely* type of situation in which you will find yourself. If material you read in this text at times appears to be contradictory, it is only because of the sometimes overlapping profiles of offenders, *not* a mistake in the text. (There are numerous texts describing sexual offenders listed in the bibliography in the back of this book.)

This book is written as a starting place for the interview process of the victims of these crimes. Most of the text is broken into general age ranges of victims of sexual assault. These age ranges are approximate only, and are merely guidelines to follow during the course of your contacts with the victims.

INTERVIEW REPORTS - CONFIDENTIALITY

Some states have laws to help protect the identity of sexual assault victims. Typically, these laws may require that law enforcement personnel conceal the name, address, etc. of all sexual assault victims so that the suspects cannot gain access to this information. Because of these new laws, most law enforcement agencies have initiated a protocol for protecting the identity of the victim, and have implemented various systems to keep the victim's identity confidential. I prefer to assign a number to each victim. For that reason, in the dialog/narrative portions of this text, victims are identified using numbers rather than their full names.

However, in cases involving "in-family" types of molestation and/or sexual assault in which all of the participants are already known to each other, and where there are multiple victims, I assign a confidential number to the primary victim and, when listing that number on the crime report face sheet, in the "victim" portion, list the number and the first name of the victim - i.e.: "97-123-Bill." This way the report will comply with these new confidentiality laws since it does not divulge personal information of the victims, yet aids the officer in being able to quickly identify the source of the information and to distinguish between victims.

Chapter 2

INTERVIEWING CHILDREN AGES 2-7

It is possible to obtain a great deal of information from a very young child, regardless of their limited verbal skills. When it comes to interviewing very young child victims, the techniques are basically the same as when interviewing older children with minor variations due to their age. When dealing with a two-year-old, however, the attention span is obviously much shorter, so they will require more frequent breaks during the interview process than older children. However, building a criminal case based solely on the statements of a child this young is almost impossible. If a child has had preschool education and/or is very mature for his/her age, you can obviously gain more information. Nonetheless, a young child's ability to qualify as a witness is always limited.

Any successful criminal prosecution is going to be based primarily on witness statements and physical evidence. Identifying and interviewing witnesses who may have actually observed the molestation or taken some spontaneous statements from the child and/or suspect are very important to document. Additionally, the medical examination by trained personnel will be very important in establishing the elements of the crime.

Children who have been molested may give many nonverbal clues that *something traumatic* has happened to them. For example, a child that has been toilet-trained may regress to wetting the bed. They might begin having severe and repeated nightmares or may line up their stuffed animals around their bed or at the bedroom door as symbolic defenders in an attempt to keep the offender away. They may refuse to go to a baby-sitter or a relative's house where they had enjoyed going to in the past.

Caution should be used and no rush to judgments made solely on the existence of any of these activities. None of these behaviors in and of themselves prove that a child has been molested. There may be other reasons for these behaviors. The investigating officer should question the family of the child to determine whether or not any of these behavior changes have been noted by the family members, when they occurred, what statements the child has made, if any, during the behavior and include that information in their report.

BACKGROUND INFORMATION

I have never interviewed a child without having some background as to what allegedly had taken place. This information usually comes from the parent, school teacher, nurse, doctor, social worker, or somebody who has already had some contact with the child. Typically, the child will have disclosed some information to one of these individuals before you would be notified. It may be as simple as the child having told their teacher that the stepfather has been touching their "private places" at bath time. This type of information gives you a very valuable head start. The suspect has been identified, and the information given to the secondary person by the child has given you an idea as to the extent of the molestation.

A more typical source of background information is when a parent brings a child in for an interview. In this case, the child has told the parent about the victimization and you will have a better picture of the extent of the molestation, including the identity of the actual suspect. Such information as the name of the perpetrator, their age, address, physical description, etc. can be gained from the adult who gives you this background information.

While this is valuable information, you have to be careful not to lead the victim through the interview based on the statements given to you by other parties. Since the person obtaining the background information is not skilled or trained in interviewing children with regard to sexual assault, they frequently added their interpretation as to what the child is saying to the description they are giving to you. It is doubtful that the person getting the background information will have clarified with the child such issues as whether or not the touching was over the clothing or skin-to-skin, or if it occurred once or multiple times.

I prefer to interview the adult AFTER I have spoken with the child for two reasons. First, it makes the interview with the child "cleaner," eliminating the perception that I led the child through the interview based on the history given by the adult. Second, when I "get it all" from the child, it eliminates the need to obtain a detailed (hearsay) statement from the adult. In this situation, the initial overview/background statement from the adult is all that is needed. (The exception to this would be a fresh complaint statement made by the child, which is discussed later.)

FIRST CONTACT WITH THE CHILD USING THE STICK FIGURE SYSTEM (SFS)

Children ages 2-7 accept the world as it is presented to them. There is really no need to go through any lengthy introductions explaining who you are or why you are there to talk with the child. This information is usually too complex for the child to understand, and wastes valuable time. It is more important to make an immediate contact with the child so that the rapport building process can take place, thus not wasting any of the limited amount of minutes you have to speak with the child.

This is best done by giving the kid a "high five" as soon as you make contact. Every child I have ever spoken to (over 1,000) understands the concept of giving someone a "high five." If they don't, it's a very simple thing to teach them.

The next thing you ask is, "How old are you?" No matter what their response is, you always tell them they look "much bigger than the average kid that age." For psychological reasons, children like to think they are larger (or smarter, or prettier, or faster) than others of their same age. I simply reinforce that needed perception in my statement and give them some additional self-confidence.

You can also ask them if they attend preschool. The preschool information can be very valuable to you as to how easy it will be to establish future rapport with the child. Every kid who has been in preschool has done a lot of drawing and learning activities generated around working in a one-on-one situation with an adult.

PHYSICAL SETTING FOR THE INTERVIEW

My experience has shown that the dinner table is the best place to conduct such an interview. In most households, the dinner table is not only where meals are served, but it is where most family business is conducted. It gives you a place to sit and a table to use for writing notes. The child is comfortable sitting at the dinner table and this is a natural environment for them to sit and talk to adults.

Contrary to popular belief, "child-friendly environments" really do not assist in producing a lot of factual information for a police report. Child-friendly environments are very good for conducting therapy or for school settings, but when it comes to conducting a factual "what happened" type of interview, the kitchen table is the best location for a comfortable discussion.

Do not have the child sitting *across* the table from you when you conduct the interview. It creates an artificial barrier between you and the child. *Instead, sit at the corner of the table.* If you are right- handed, sit with the child at 90 degrees from you on your left side. This allows you to write and draw with the child without your arm blocking the child's view of what you are doing. Left-handed? Simply reverse the seating, staying at the corners of the table. (Refer to following illustration)

(Fig. 1) Seating arrangement for interviewing a child.

Don't be afraid to sit close to the child, or be concerned if the child wants to touch your uniform. They are naturally curious at this age and simple touching won't hurt your uniform. If you are successful in making a good connection with the child, by the end of the interview, the child may be sitting in your lap helping you draw while discussing the actual molestation allegations.

If the child wants a parent present during the interview, that is acceptable. However, be sure to limit it to only one parent, and also try to keep other children and family members from interrupting the interview process.

RAPPORT BUILDING

This is accomplished very simply. Take any piece of standard size paper, such as the continuation page for a crime report, or the diagram page from a traffic accident report or any other paper that allows you enough blank space on which to draw. You can then begin to engage the child in a "comfort building" activity.

Ask the child if he or she knows how to "trace hands." If the child has been in preschool, they have done this many times in the past; if not, it's an easy thing to teach. *You* first trace one hand of the child by putting their hand on the piece of paper and using your pen to outline their fingers. Next, have the child outline your hand on the same piece of paper. If the child is very young, you may have to help them actually hold the pen as they trace your fingers. These drawings may be a bit crude, but they are not intended for museum submission. They are simply great bonding exercises. The drawing may be left with the child to display on the refrigerator when you leave, or you may discard them (out of the child's presence) after the end of the interview. Whatever the ultimate fate of the drawings, the exercise develops a bond and begins of the process of you and the child *working together*. (Refer to following illustration)

(Fig. 2) Hand Tracings

IDENTIFYING BODY PARTS

Now that you have established a rapport with the child using the hand tracing exercises, you are ready to move on to the identification of body parts using a more refined drawing exercise. Because of vocabulary limitations of a child of this age, you need to establish that you are talking the same language when it comes to identifying physical anatomy. This is done quite easily by drawing a stick figure on another piece of paper incorporating the Stick Figure System which *will* be maintained as evidence. (Refer to following illustration)

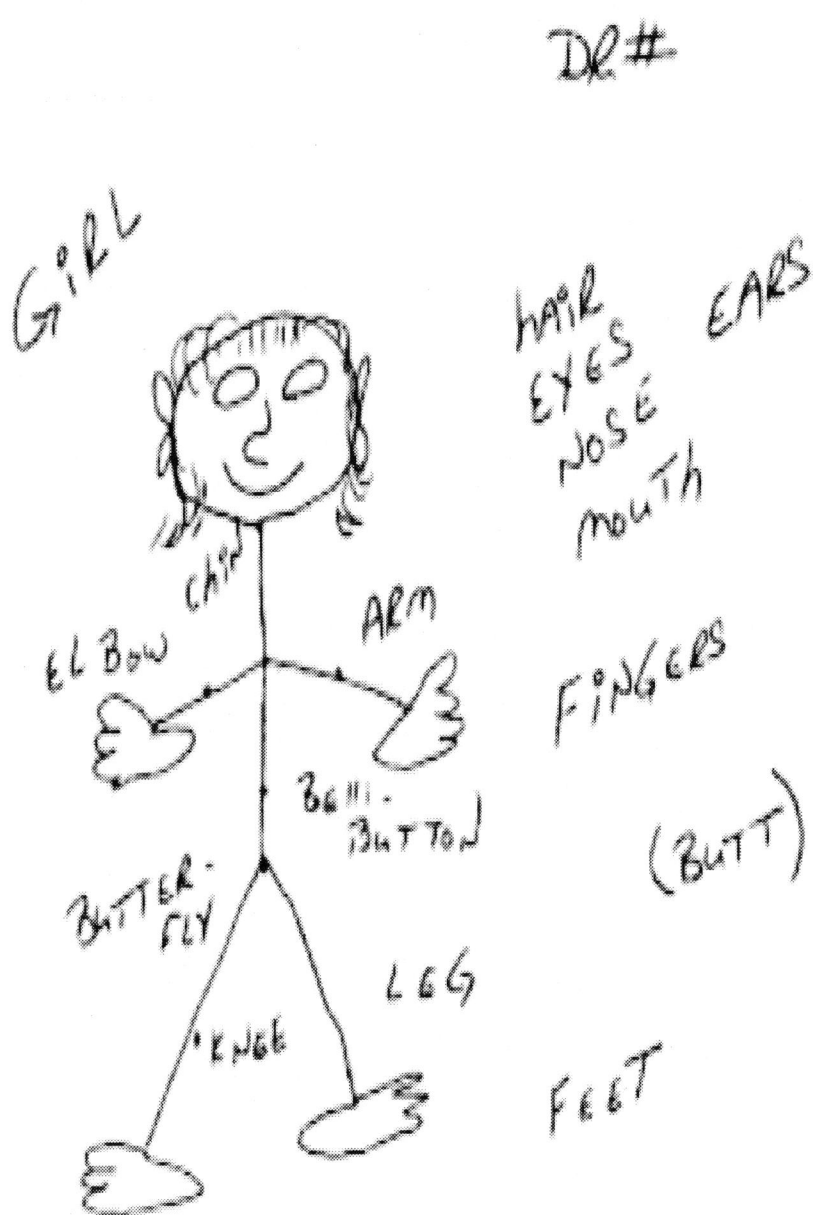

(Fig. 3) Stick Figure identifying body parts.

As you start this process, ask the child, "Can you help me draw a people?" For some reason, the word "people" creates an immediate bond between you and the child. They know you speak their language. Always be sure to use the word, "people" as opposed to "person," "individual," "man" or "woman."

Ask the child if they want to draw a boy or a girl "people." In my experience, the child usually chooses the same sex drawing that they are. You label the piece of paper "girl" (if that is the case) and you begin to draw the stick figure. As you draw a large circle for the head, you tell the child, "I don't draw people very good, so don't laugh at me, okay?" Again, this is a real rapport builder between you and the child and the child is now working with you as you continue the stick figure.

Next, draw a single line down from the circle to represent the body, "Y" shaped lines at the base of the body to indicate the legs, and then two stick arms out to the side.

You now begin the process of working with the child to fill in the stick figure drawing. You start with the top of the drawing and ask the child to identify what else is needed to make the stick figure look like a real "people." You may have to point to the child's nose and ask her what that is in order for her to understand the concept. Once you point to the nose, you draw in the nose and label it on the side of the drawing as "nose." You do the same thing for mouth, ears, eyes, etc. You can also ask the child if they want to make this person happy or sad. If the child wants it to be a happy person, then you make a smiling face; for a sad person, draw a frown.

As you continue down the body, ask the child to identify the hands, elbows, knees, feet, etc. As you do so, you label each of these body parts off to the side as the child gives you the name for them. If the child identifies the hands as being "fingers," then you write down "fingers". If she identifies the feet as being "toes," or "shoes," you write those words.

After you have identified hands, elbows, knees, feet, you go to the area of the navel. In every case I have had, the child has always referred to the navel as a "belly button." After identifying that part of the body, you point to the groin area of the drawing. Normally, the child will immediately respond with whatever they call that part of the body. A girl may refer to this part of the body as her "vagina," "twinkie," "butterfly," "pee-pee" or other such names. Whatever term she uses, write that word to the side of the drawing. If you are interviewing a boy, he will most likely identify the genitals as being his "penis," "wiener," "pee-pee," etc. If the child gives an

"X-rated" term for body parts, write that down also, and continue the interviewing process without commenting on the term given for the genitals.

After identifying the genitals, simply turn the paper over quickly and ask the child what would a person have on the back part of their body in that same general area. The child should respond with their "butt," "bottom" or other such term. After determining their term for the buttock area, turn the paper back over and start to identify other parts of the body. At this time, I usually point to the neck, chin or arm in order to get the child to identify some other body parts so as not to immediately focus on the genitals.

If you are speaking to a girl, you will want to go back to the genital area and ask the child, "what does a boy have in this area?" Hopefully, the girl will identify a boy's body parts as being his "penis," "wiener" or something similar. The same is true if you are interviewing a boy. Ask him what a girl has in that area, and hopefully, he will respond with something that is a common term used for a girl's genitals.

If the child appears to be reluctant to tell you what the family name is for private parts of their body, it is okay for the parent (who is sitting in on the interview) to prompt the child with that term. The child will translate this into the parent giving permission for them to continue with identifying the rest of their body parts.

Once you have identified the body parts, it is an easy step to start asking about any touching of the genitals, who is doing the touching, and under what circumstances. (The procedure is discussed in the next section.)

PRE-DRAWN ANATOMY

Some police departments and social service agencies use pre-drawn pictures of people. These pre-drawn figures are used to help identify body parts, much the same way that the Stick Figure System does. There are several different types of drawings in use. Some are more anatomically correct than others are and some are more like cartoon characters.

The negative side for law enforcement is that cops have enough stuff to carry around as it is and the idea of having a handful of naked people drawings mixed in with your crime reports, traffic accident forms and vehicle impounds doesn't appeal to most cops. Also, they eliminate the spontaneity of the interaction between the officer and the child. You may lose some very interesting evidentiary type statements by the child if they are not interacting with you as completely as they have to do with the Stick

Figure System. The pre-drawn figures also imply that all people look alike.

On the positive side, they are a quick way to identify body parts without introducing a play element into your forensic interview. One word of warning, be sure to watch the child's reaction to the drawings. Some families teach that any form of nudity is wrong and/or embarrassing. So, if the child turns away from the drawings or seems suddenly shy, put the drawings away and draw a Stick Figure.

Many times I've met with a social worker who has already interviewed a child using the pre-drawn figures. In these cases there's no need to start over with a different method. Simply use the drawings to review body part identification and continue with the rest of the interview. Remember, under California law, only the police officer can testify at the preliminary hearing for the child, and only to information he/she received directly from the child.

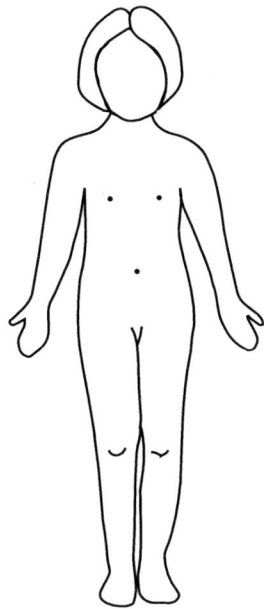

(Fig. 4) Pre-drawn girl anatomy

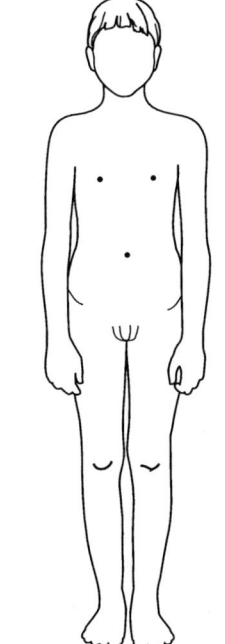

(Fig. 5) Pre-drawn boy anatomy

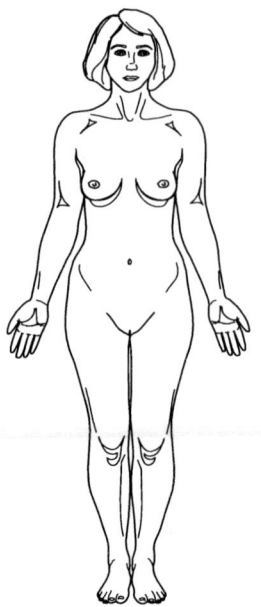

(Fig. 6) Predrawn adult female anatomy

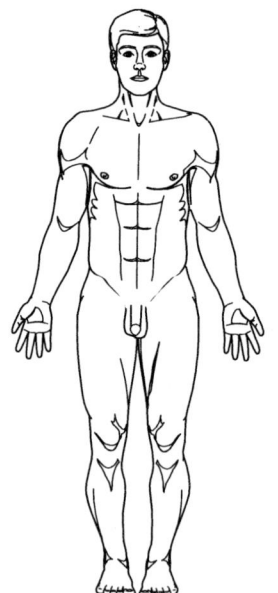

(Fig. 7) Predrawn adult male anatomy

USE OF ANATOMICALLY CORRECT DOLLS

Several years ago, the use of anatomically correct dolls was quite the rage in law enforcement for interviewing children. However, it was found that these dolls were too suggestive since they are the only type of dolls the child would ever see that actually have genitals attached to the body. Because of this, the child has a tendency to focus in on those genitals as opposed to carrying on a conversation with you. Because of that, anatomically correct dolls are rarely used by law enforcement today.

If a child is stumbling over a term for a body part, or simply can't describe what actually happened, you may want to use one of the child's own dolls to give them a tool to describe where the person touched them.

GOOD TOUCH VS. BAD TOUCH

If the child is verbal enough, you might ask them if they know the difference between a good touch and a bad touch. If they aren't sure, you can explain to them that a good touch is something that is caring or comforting, like a hug. A bad touch would be something that is secret, or hurts, or makes them feel uncomfortable, like being hit or pinched. This leads you right into the questioning of the child that asks, "Has anyone ever touched you in a bad way?"

QUALIFYING AS A WITNESS

The general rule of law is that a witness is considered qualified to testify in court unless there is some information to make the court feel that the witness does not know the difference between the truth and a lie. Sometimes, this will come up in a courtroom setting where someone, usually the defense attorney, will want to know if the child knows or is able to express the difference between telling the truth and telling a lie, or the difference between right and wrong.

In California, the interviewing police officers are now allowed to testify at the preliminary hearing on behalf of the victim. (CA Code of Civil Proc. Sec. 872 - see your individual state laws.) You are going to have to be able to tell the court that you established the concept of truth versus non-truth with the witness during the time that you interviewed them. There is a very simple way to do that. Normally, what you do is point at the child's shirt and ask them what color it is. If the shirt is blue, you ask the child, *"If I were to say that the shirt was red, instead of blue, would that be the truth, or would it be a lie?"* Hopefully, the child would respond by saying, *"That would be a lie,"* or, *"That would be silly,"* or *"That would be stupid,"* etc. You then ask the child, *"Are you supposed to tell a lie, or are you supposed to tell the truth?"* The child should respond by saying, *"You're supposed to tell the truth."* You then ask the child, *"What happens when you tell a lie?"* The child should respond by saying, *"I'm put in time-out,"* or *"Mama gets mad at me."* This establishes that the child knows the difference between right and wrong, between telling the truth and a lie, and that there are consequences to telling lies.

ATTENTION SPAN

The younger the child, the shorter their attention span. I have seen many interviewers work a child far past their ability to concentrate on one particular subject. You, as an interviewer, have to understand the limitations of the child. In very general terms, a child between the ages of four and seven years will have an attention span initially of perhaps four to eight minutes.

After that four-to-eight minute time span, you will notice that the child becomes fidgety and is not concentrating as well as in the beginning. You need to take the child off of the subject of the molestation for approximately 45 seconds to one minute. Any longer than that, and the child will become too absorbed in the new subject matter and will not want to come back to the subject of the molestation. (There will be further discussion as to how to do this in subsequent sections.)

After this 45 second to one-minute break from the primary subject, you bring the child back on topic for perhaps two or three more minutes. After the two or three-minute additional interview time, the child will start to show signs of fatigue and it will be necessary for you to take them off subject for approximately another minute or so.

After this second break from the primary interview subject, you will have an opportunity to bring them back on subject for perhaps a minute or two to ask some cleanup type questions before the child's attention span has been lost altogether. If you try to interview the child beyond their attention span, they will begin to talk about things that will be completely out of context of the subject you are talking about. Be sure not to fatigue the child or interview them past their ability to intelligently respond to you.

NUMBER OF COUNTS

During the course of the interview, you will need to try to establish the number of times that a criminal act took place. If the child is very young, you may only get a statement such as, "it happened a few times" versus "it happened a lot of times." The child may be able to say that it happened four or five times. If they give you an exact number, such as "five," ask them to count to five, so you can be sure they understand that concept.

With younger children, they may tell you that the molestation took place "every time I was at Grandpa's house," or other such statements. To clarify that type of time frame/count statement, the parent of the child can tell you that they went to visit Grandpa every weekend, or every other weekend for the last six months, which will give you a time frame so that the District Attorney's Office can file criminal counts at a later time.

California, and some other states, allow a prosecutor to file a generalized count of child molest in situations where a child has been molested over time, by a child care provider, when individual criminal counts cannot be established. However, it is still better from a criminal prosecution point of view to tie down the exact number of counts and file them individually. (There will be further discussion of that issue in the next chapter.)

TIME FRAMES

The rule of law is that you have to provide the suspect/defendant with an opportunity to say that he was out of town on the day that the alleged crime took place. Therefore, it is important to tie down, as accurately as possible, a general time as to when the crime took place. This may be as simple as the child saying; "it happened during Christmas vacation," or "it happened right after school started," or "it happened during the summer," or "it happened at the beach party," etc.

SECRETS

Sometime during the course of the interview, you should ask the child if he or she was asked to keep the molestation secret. If so, you need to explain to the child the difference between a "good secret" and a "bad secret, and that it's okay to tell "bad secrets." You will also want to ask the child what they were told the consequences would be for telling the "bad secret," such as "you'll get into trouble," or, "grandpa will never be able to see you again," or, "the police department will come and take you away." Once aware of the threats, you can minimize the child's fear of telling by explaining what will *happen* and that grownups are responsible for what they do, not the kids. This eliminates the child's fear that they will be in trouble.

OTHER VICTIMS

You should also ask the victim if he or she is aware of any other children that are being victimized. Sometimes, the children have actually witnessed siblings or other neighbor children being molested, and you want to try to identify those children.

DOING IT CORRECTLY

You'll know that you're doing it correctly when the kids start leaving their chair to sit in your lap. Usually, they want to draw something for you, so give them a new piece of paper and let them draw whatever they want. *Don't let them scribble on the evidence.* (The stick figure drawing will be booked into evidence later.)

INTERVIEW OF CHILD 2-7 YEARS USING THE STICK FIGURE SYSTEM

You receive a radio call to "see the woman" with regard to a child molestation investigation. The radio call indicates that the reporting party, the child's mother, is stating that the child has been molested during a weekend visitation at the child's father's home; it also indicates that the suspect is the father's roommate.

When you arrive at the scene, you find that the mother is holding the five-year-old in her arms. You approach both mom and the child and you hold out your hand so that child can give you a "high five," while asking the child their age and telling them that they are "big for their age." You then speak very briefly with the mother to obtain the background information to confirm that it is the biological father's roommate who is the suspect and that the last molestation would have occurred a few days prior, during the last visitation.

Since the child will accept the world as it is presented to them, there is no need to carry on any extensive introductions between yourself and the child. Instead, simply tell the mother that you want to talk with the child at the dinner table, and enter the house to do just that. As described earlier, position yourself so that you and the child are sitting at the corner of the table.

Due to the age of the child, it is perfectly acceptable to have the mother present during this interview, but have her sitting across the table from you, as opposed to between you and the child. Never stand towering over the child, since this is an intimidating posture and the child is not likely to talk to you.

The next thing you do is trace hands with the child. First, trace the child's hand, then have the child trace your hand. In your police report, this hand tracing is referred to as "rapport building." The actual sketches of the hands do not need to be maintained as evidence.

You then ask the child to draw the stick figure with you, where you identify the body parts. Usually, I do the drawing, but if the child wants to actually draw in the hands, eyes, nose, let them do so. During this process, tell the child that if they don't know the answer to something, then it is okay for them to say, *"I don't know."* Giving them this option makes the interview "non-leading and non-suggestive."

Drawing with the child in this fashion helps build the interaction between you and the child. It also gives you an idea of how capable the child is in understanding concepts and what level of vocabulary you can use when talking with the child.

These initial interaction steps have nothing to do with the actual interview about the molestation itself. As a result, you have not infringed on the attention span of the child with reference as to how long the child will be able to talk to you about the actual molestation allegation.

Now, here's how the actual questioning about the molestation would transpire. After the stick figure has been completed, ask the child if it's "okay for someone to touch them on their hair." Hopefully, the child will say "yes." You might ask them if it's okay to touch them on the hands, and you can reach over and touch the child on the hand at the same time. And again you hope the child will say "yes." You then point to the genitals on the stick figure and ask the child if it's okay if someone touches them on their vagina. If the child says "no" you just continue on with other body parts to see if the child continues to state appropriate responses as to whether or not it's okay to be touched on the toes, feet, ankles, knees, etc.

Then go back to the genitals and ask if someone has ever touched them "there." If they answer "yes" then ask them who it was. The child should immediately respond with the first name of the suspect, e.g., Bill. Then ask the child a question that will identify the relationship of this child to the suspect, such as, "Where does this person live?" "Is this person a family member, like an uncle or cousin?" That is normally about all the identifying information you will be able to get from a child this age.

Ask the child if this touching was part of a game they were playing, or if "Bill" was being "mean." If the child indicates that it was a game, you ask them what the name of the game was. Normally, they will say, "truth or dare," or "playing doctor." If "Bill was being mean," ask the child to explain this.

A third possibility is that the child was touched during bath time, or while the person was helping them get dressed, etc. If so, try to get the child to elaborate on that. Often, a parent assumes that any touching of their child's genitals was done as part of a molestation. However, the elements of a crime require that the child be touched "with the intent to sexually arouse either the child or the adult." If the touching took place as part of an attempt at hygiene or during the bathing process, you may not have a crime. The elements of a crime are usually met if the touching had no legitimate purpose.

You continue by asking the child if this has happened "a lot of times," or "a few times," and try to get the child to count for you or show you on her fingers how many times the molestation took place. You also have to ask the child if this touching took place over the clothing or "skin to skin." The way you do this is by asking the child, "Did you have your clothes on, or clothes off when it happened?" Also ask if the suspect had his clothes on or clothes off at the time this took place.

If dealing with a female victim, you now have to ask if there was any penetration of the vaginal area. Since the child will have no frame of reference as to what "inside" means versus "outside" of her body, this is a very difficult concept to get across to the child. I have found that the easiest way to do this is to use the index and middle finger on your left hand to represent the child's vagina, and then the index finger on your other hand to represent the suspect's hand or penis. You then take the right hand index finger and rub it on the outside of the other two fingers and ask the child, "Did he touch you on the *outside*?" while demonstrating, or, "Did he touch you on the *inside*?" while placing one index finger between the other two fingers. (Refer to the following illustration) This has been the best way that I have found to get the child to understand the concept of what "inside her body" might mean.

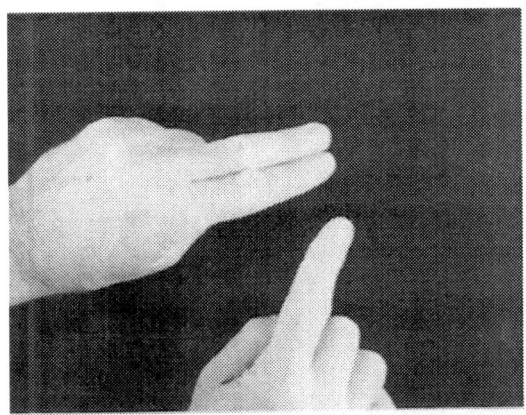
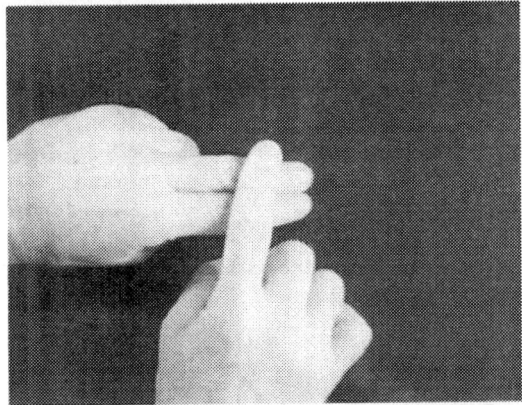
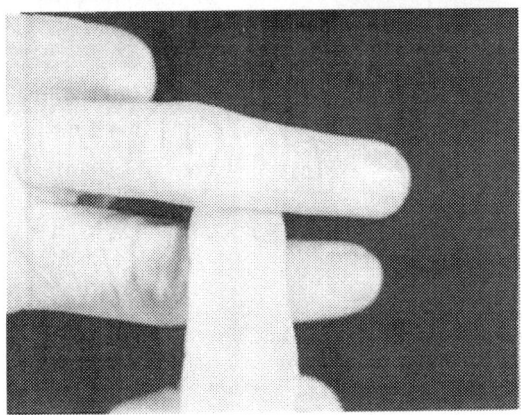

(Fig. 8) Use of fingers to illustrate vaginal touching

You should also ask the child what she was touched with. Don't assume that the touching was done with the hands or the genitals of the adult. Again, you do this by referring back to the stick figure, and ask, "Did Bill touch you with his fingers?" while pointing to the hands, or "Did he touch you with his nose, or with his tongue, or his mouth, or his penis, or his feet?"

By now, you will have used up the first four or eight minutes of your interview time with the child. The four to eight minute "clock" starts when the child states that their genitals were touched. As a result, you take them off subject by asking questions that will determine their qualification as a witness.

Point to their clothing and ask them, "Is that a blue shirt you're wearing?" " If I were to say that shirt is red, instead of blue, would that be the truth, or would that be a lie?" " Are you supposed to tell the truth or are you supposed to lie?" "What happens if you lie?" etc. This qualifying the child as a witness should take about a minute and suffices for taking the child's mind off of the molestation interview while, at the same time, not allowing them to become so engrossed in some other play activity where you cannot get them back on subject.

You can now determine if the suspect was naked. You do this by asking the child, "Did he have his clothes on, or his clothes off?" If the suspect was naked, you ask the child if she saw the suspect's penis. If the answer is yes, you have to ask if his penis was erect or non-erect. This is an important issue since it goes to show the sexual intent of the crime. Obviously, if the suspect is standing naked with an erection in front of a small child, it shows some sort of sexual intent on their part. Again, you have to demonstrate this with a child. You take your index finger and, in a hook shape, you show the child and ask the child, "Was his penis hanging down like this or was it sticking out straight?" Bend your finger down then stick it out straight, as a way of demonstrating the flaccid and the erect penis. Normally, the child will indicate that the penis was sticking out straight.

CHAPTER 2

INTERVIEWING CHILDREN AGES 2-7

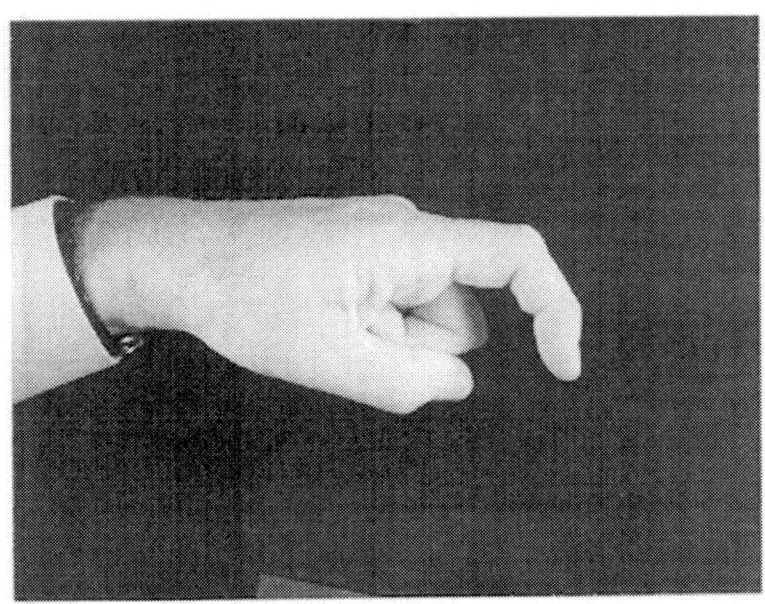

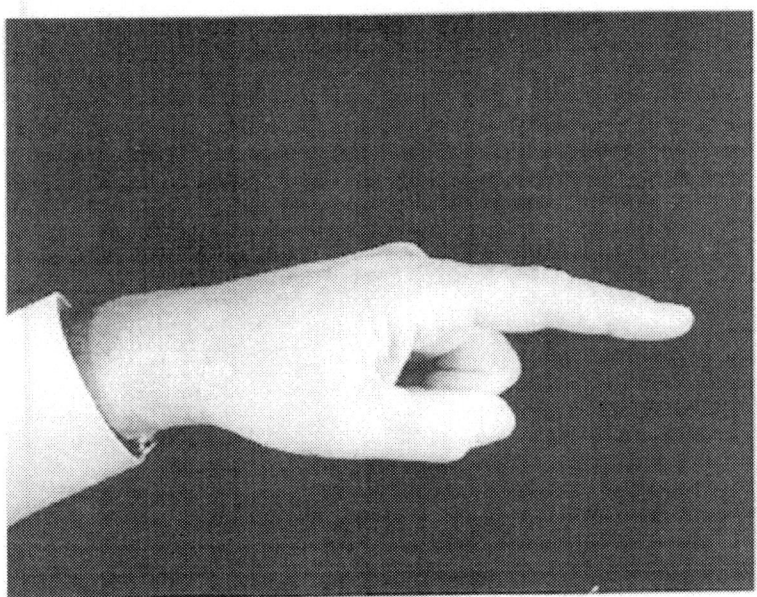

(Fig. 9) Use of fingers to to illustrate flaccid and erect

Another method is to ask the child to give you an idea as to the size of the suspect's penis by taking my two index fingers and indicating, "Is it real small, like this size?" (illustrating by putting your index fingers close together) or, "Is it real big?" (by putting your fingers, perhaps, several feet apart or somewhere in between). If the child is old enough to understand this concept, the child will generally put their two index fingers at a distance that will proximate the length of the suspect's penis. You then have the child put those two fingers down on the piece of paper that you have used to do the stick figure, and make a mark between the two fingers and later measure that distance to see how long the suspect's penis is. (Refer to the following illustration.) You might want to go so far as to have the child draw what the suspect's penis looks like. I have done this on several occasions and have gotten remarkably accurate representations of the suspect's penis. This is also a drawing that you should maintain as evidence.

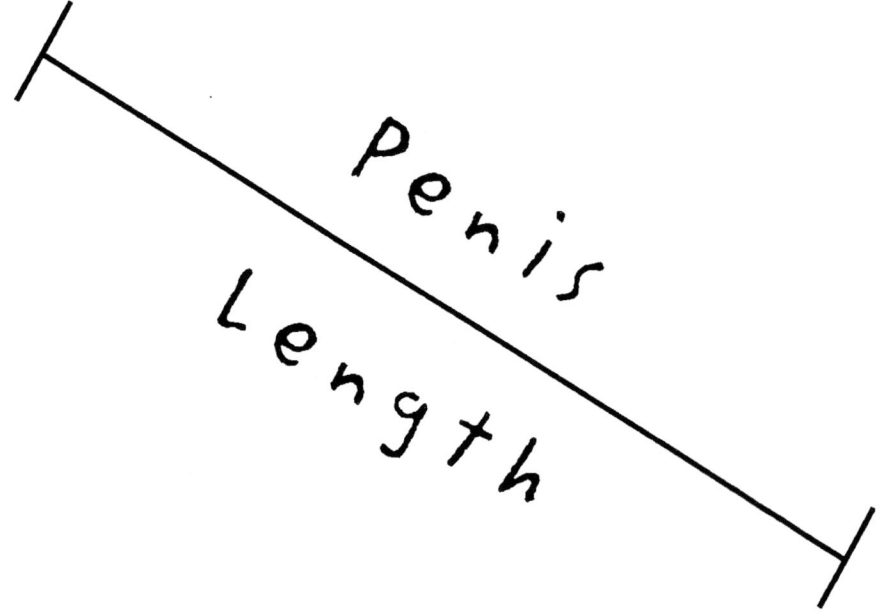

(Fig. 10) Estimated penis length drawing

CHAPTER 2　　　　　　　　　　　　　　　INTERVIEWING CHILDREN AGES 2-7

Doing it this way will often generate some very interesting evidence items. I have had cases in which the children have drawn the suspect's penis to be very short and very curved, only to find out later that the suspect's genitals had been misshaped at birth and actually were deformed, as drawn by the child. The child might also draw some sort of tattooing or scarring, etc. around the genitals. This is one of the advantages to having the child interact with you by drawing the stick figure with you as opposed to using pre-drawns which may lead the child to an assumption that everybody's body looks the same.

Obviously, the older the child is, the more detail they will be able to give you about the suspect's genitals and the greater length of time you will have to interview the child on this subject.

At about this time, the child typically becomes fatigued again and you may be beginning to lose their attention. If you see this happening, take them off subject for a short time. This is an excellent opportunity to take a break and ask them about their family. Specifically, ask them how many brothers and sisters they have, if the siblings are older or younger, what their names are, and if anyone else lives in their home, such as mother, father, aunt or uncle. This type of questioning should last for perhaps one to two minutes before you again bring the child back to the subject of the molestation. To allow them to do so for any longer would result in you "losing them."

Now, you will have a final opportunity to bring them back on subject for perhaps a minute or two to conduct some "cleanup" questions. These questions normally consist of a description as to where and when the molestation actually took place. Ask the child what room it took place in, such as the bedroom, kitchen or living room. Was it daytime or nighttime? Was it weekend or weekday? Was anyone else present? Did it happen on the bed, the floor, in the chair, etc.? (Young children respond best to short, closed questions and can easily give you one-or-two word responses.)

These are very important questions because if the child has been molested, they should be able to give you some of these associated details as to the environment surrounding the actual molestation. It could be as simple as the child stating that they were lying in bed when the suspect came in, pulled the covers off of them, and then fondled them. The child simply relating that the covers were removed from their body is an associated detail that helps establish that they were actually present when this happened and are relating factual details about what actually took place.

That is about all of the actual interview time you are going to have with the child. By now, the child is bored with the subject matter and only wants to play or draw, or talk about something other than the molestation allegation. You would now want to conduct some follow-up questions with the child's mother to further identify the suspect, find out how long that person has been a roommate of the biological father, how much she might know about him, where he works, what his phone number is, and similar types of identifying questions. I have included a comprehensive **Interview Checklist** for your convenience. (*See page*)

FALSE REPORTS

With children of this age, sometimes you will get a false report. Generally it involves information given to the child by one parent who is in the middle of a heated custody dispute with the other parent. Children of this age really don't have the ability to lie. Lying implies an intent to deceive someone with some sort of purpose or reason to gain something by telling the lie. Children of this age really don't lie, even though they may say things that are not true. The easiest example of this is if a four-year-old tells you that Santa Claus came down the chimney last night and left Christmas presents under the tree. The child really is not lying to you, but at the same time, they are not saying something that they know to be true.

Sometimes, in a custody battle or divorce situation, one parent might actually coach the child to make up an allegation of molestation, or that parent will exaggerate what the child has stated about some touching that occurred during a weekend visitation. In this type of situation, the child will not be able to tell you the associated details of the molestation, such as: was the touching "good touching" or "bad touching?" Did it happen during the daytime or nighttime? Were the clothes on or the clothes off, etc.? That is why the interview process as described earlier is very important, since it does not imply the answers to any of the questions that you are asking the child.

It also allows you to discover if there has been a misinterpretation of the child's statement to the adult. The adult has interpreted the situation to indicate that there has been some sort of molestation when, in essence, there was no molestation. The touching was simply a part of some sort of hygiene problem, or did not happen at all.

After you have done several child molestation interviews, a "bad" case will stand out like a sore thumb. After a while, you will learn how a child normally relates a molestation incident to you and the type of details that a child should be able to give you about a molestation. When you find an interview that does not meet these normal standards that you are accustomed to seeing, you might suspect that there is a false report situation involved. You then need to ask the child's parent if there are any custody or other related problems between them.

REPEATING QUESTIONS

Children assume that adults know more than they do. For this reason, if you ask a child a question over and over again, the child will assume that they have given the wrong answer. They will assume this because had they given the right answer, an adult would *stop* asking the question. If you repeatedly ask a child the same question over and over again, they will change their answer. This does not mean they are lying to you; it is simply a part of the child abuse accommodation syndrome (a phrase coined after extensive research, teaching and writings by Dr. Roland Summit- see Ch. 7 and Bibliography). It is very common in young children. Defense attorneys are very aware of this and that is why they will ask a child the same question over and over again in an attempt to get them to change their answer. You, as an interviewer, have to be aware of this. Be sure that you don't ask the same question over and over again, because this will simply confuse the child and result in you getting conflicting responses.

What if the child says "no" about being touched? The answer is quite simple. What you do is simply ask the child what they are supposed to do if someone does touch them. You go over the safety rules, such as: say no and run and tell someone. You then ask the child to repeat the safety rules to you, and then you ask the child one more time if anyone has touched them on their genitals. If the child says, "no," then the interview is over. Remember that "no" is the preferable answer. Discovering that a child has not been molested is preferable to finding out that they have been. This system is designed to discover if the molestation has actually occurred or not.

TAPE-RECORDING / VIDEOTAPING

In my opinion, there is no need to tape-record or videotape any victim interview, either with a child or an adult. There is nothing in law that requires us to tape anything. Police officers do not routinely videotape burglary victims or robbery victims, and I don't see why we need to tape-record child victims. I know that there are several different opinions in this regard, and that some agencies, especially some of the social service agencies, believe that videotaping is the right thing to do. Personally, I have found that this is more of a hindrance than a help.

The initial idea of videotaping or audio-taping the child victims was to eliminate the need for a child to be re-interviewed many times by different people throughout the protective services, protective custody and social services process. However, I have found that this is actually not the case. If you, as a the interviewer, *get all of the information, get it right, and get it the first time,* then that is sufficient as far as the details of the molestation that took place. By recording interviews, we have spoiled the defense attorneys. Since some agencies have routinely begun videotaping and audio-taping child molestation victims, there is an assumption that this is the standard practice and that there is some legal reason to do it. This is far from the truth.

The idea of videotaping and audio-taping child victims was sort of a knee-jerk response to poor interviews that were being conducted by law enforcement. It was thought that if you use some technical wizardry to record the interview with the child, this would somehow make that interview with the child better. In reality, if you tape-record a poor interview with a child, then you have made the situation worse, as opposed to better. If you follow the simple formula outlined earlier in your interview with the child, you should be able to *get all of the information* you need from the child, you *get it all correctly,* and you *get it all the first time.* Then there is really no need for a videotape or an audio-tape.

I have heard several people talk about success stories where playing the videotape forced the suspect to confess to a crime. I'm sure that's true, but I have many success stories where I have gotten suspects to confess to crimes where nothing was taped. I also know several horror stories in which the taping equipment failed and the interviewer forgot to take notes and has no clear recollection of the interview itself, because he thought the tape was going to capture the interview.

I have also seen many videotapes of policemen trying to interview children in child-friendly environments. One that stands out was an interviewer trying to talk to a teenage girl about having been molested for several years by her stepfather. The child-friendly environment that this police department had developed was two beanbag chairs sitting on the floor in an interview room that had a large clock mounted at floor level. This way, the camera, which was across the room, could actually monitor the time that the interview was taking place. However, the two people (the interviewer and the child) had to sit on opposite sides of the clock on these rather clumsy beanbag chairs. The tape of the interview clearly shows how the overweight and out of shape officer had trouble getting in and out of the beanbag chair, and how the girl spent most of the interview making sure that her legs were crossed so that the video would not show what was up her dress. Also, since they had to keep the clock between the two of them, there was no way for the two to interact at all, nor was there any way for the officer to take notes.

Trust me. Sit at the kitchen table, get all of the information, follow the method, (SFS) and you will be light years ahead of anyone who thinks that an interview can be improved upon by simply taping it.

TEAMING WITH SOCIAL SERVICES

Frequently, there will be a situation in which the social worker will want you to meet them at the home or school so they can conduct their interview at the same time you do. This is perfectly acceptable. There is no need to exclude the social worker from your interview. I have never experienced a problem where a social worker was called into court to be a witness where any sort of contradictory statements were made. The police officer has to remember, however, that he is in charge of the interview and he has the primary responsibility for obtaining the investigative information and for making a decision as to what type of crime report should be taken. The officer determines if the child should be taken into protective custody and if arrests should be made. The social worker should have some input into these decisions, but the ultimate decision and responsibility lies with the police officer. However, in cases with teamed interviews with social workers, a little bit of diplomacy goes a long way.

PROTECTIVE CUSTODY

Section 300 of the California Welfare and Institutions Code (see your individual state laws) details how a child should be taken into protective custody and under what circumstances. If you, as a police officer, make the determination that the child, for their protection, needs to be taken into protective custody, then you will have to do so per your department's protocols.

Normally, all you would have to do is fill out a simple petition form and then have the actual police report either attached to that form or have it faxed or forwarded to the foster home facility within a few hours of the child actually being delivered there.

The decision to take the child into protective custody is based on whether or not the child is going to be safe remaining at home. If the child is being molested by someone inside the home, and you arrest that person and remove them from the home, the child might be safe there. However, since the person might make bail or be released on their own recognizance, that is not a simple solution to the problem.

The problem with in-family molestation situations is that frequently the non-molesting parent is not going to take steps to adequately protect the child. It is not unusual for the wife in an incest situation to coerce the child into changing their story and to make every effort possible to bring the suspect back into the home once he has promised to "never do it again." You have to make an evaluation as to whether or not the parent is going to be protective of the child. The way you assess this is by trying to find out what type of action, if any, the parent took to protect the child once the disclosure of the molestation took place. If the mother protected the child by kicking her husband out and changing the locks on the doors and threatening to kill him if he returned, then you can assume that that mother is going to take steps to protect the child. If, however, the mother did absolutely nothing, told the child to keep it "our little secret," and then apologized to the suspect for walking in on him as he was having sex with the child, then you can assume that that parent is not going to take any steps to adequately protect the child, even if the suspect is taken into custody.

Often, in an incestuous relationship, it is best to put the child in protective custody, let the social workers do an in-depth evaluation of the family dynamics, and then let them decide whether or not the child should return home.

The protective custody situation and social services, in general, is a very complex, bureaucratic environment into which you are going to introduce the child. Fortunately, most foster home facilities are very nice places for the child. However, the legal fight that generates around the child being in protective custody is quite lengthy, very involved and is outside the scope of this book.

Suffice it to say that if you *got all of the information*, and *you got it right*, and you *got it the first time*, you have done absolutely the best thing you could ever do for the child who has been molested. To document what happened as thoroughly and accurately as possible is the best thing that you, as a police officer, can do for the further protection of that child.

In all of my years as a police officer, I have never had to testify at a dependency hearing in Juvenile Court. My police reports, as yours will be, become the "gospel" for what happened to that child. If you have done an inadequate job and have not documented what actually happened to the best of your ability, it is quite possible that that child will be returned to an abusive environment. If, on the other hand, you *got all of the information, got it all right,* and *you got it all the first time,* you have done the best that you could possibly do to see to it that that child will not be returned to an abusive environment.

Following this method for interviewing children of this age allows the child to talk about a molestation issue if, in fact, one is occurring. This technique is designed to also discover if no molestation is taking place, which is equally important to establish.

ASAV: ALLEGED SEXUAL ASSAULT VICTIM EXAMINATION

"ASAV" is an acronym for Alleged Sexual Assault Victim examination. The procedure is used by hospital and nursing staff to determine the extent of sexual trauma to a victim's body when molestation or sexual assault has been alleged. The medical examination will discover any physical evidence as to vaginal or rectal injuries that will become corroborative evidence to your case.

When is it appropriate for a police officer to conduct a vaginal exam on a child? *NEVER! There is absolutely no reason for a police officer to examine the genitals of a child who has been molested.* This may sound like an over-simplification, but over the years, I have read many police reports in which an officer has conducted a vaginal exam on a three-or four-year-old to see if there is any evidence, or redness, soreness, tenderness, or swelling to the child's genitals that might be supportive evidence of the child's statement about being molested. *This is totally inappropriate.*

Not only does the medical community absolutely "flip out" when this happens, the police officer is doing exactly the same thing we are trying to send someone to prison for— touching a child's genitals when they have no business being down there.

An actual medical examination of a child's genitals, when done properly, will examine the internal structures of the child's genitalia. Redness to the outer labia/vagina is often meaningless in a molestation allegation. There are many reasons why the outer labia might be red, tender or swollen. Most of these reasons have absolutely nothing to do with being molested.

When the ASAV is conducted by qualified medical professionals, they look at the internal structures in an attempt to find thickening of the hymnal ring, any sort of tears, abrasions, etc. They will use a tool known as a colposcope to magnify the findings as a part of the internal examination of the child. They also have the medical background to render an opinion as to whether or not what they are seeing is evidence of a molestation or is normal for that child. Physicians have told me that hymens are like snowflakes…they are all unique and it takes an expert to distinguish one that has been damaged versus one that has not been. Also, because a lot of child molesting involves a simple fondling of the child with no actual penetration of the genitals or rectal area, it is not unusual for there to be no evidence, or no physical findings as a part of an ASAV examination. This negative finding, however, does not mean that a molestation did not occur.

There will be times when you go to speak to the parent of the molested child, and they will tell you that they (the parent) conducted a visual exam of the child's genitals and they saw some redness, swelling, or tenderness. You can note that in your police report as being a factual thing that they saw, but don't conclude for a minute that seeing some redness to the outer labia is any proof whatsoever that there was a molestation.

In a situation where a child has been forcibly raped and is bleeding or needs immediate medical attention, take that child to the emergency room for medical treatment. If emergency room treatment is not necessary, then follow the normal protocols for handling any rape victim. Normally, this involves taking the child to a location where a rape examination can be done so that biological samples can be obtained for evidence purposes.

In Orange County, California, the CAST (Child Abuse Services Team) services are available on a twenty-four-hour-a-day basis. The office itself is only open during normal business hours, but there is a round-the-clock call-out procedure that can be followed. When unavailable, the hospital handling adult rape victims has trained medical personnel on staff around the clock who can conduct a forensic exam of a child's genitals to collect biological evidence left by the suspect (seminal fluid) and can photograph and document any genital tearing or injuries. Most counties have similar services available to them. It's important for the investigator to be familiar with the capabilities of the various medical facilities in their local area.

An immediate exam is not needed if the molestation has been ongoing and the last incident occurred three or more days ago. In this situation, it's best to document your interview and let the assigned investigator make the decision about having a medical exam done.

INTERVIEWS AT SCHOOL

If you are called to a school to interview a child because of an allegation of molestation, it is in most cases perfectly legal to interview that child at school without the parents' permission, consent or knowledge. Obviously, if the molester is someone within the child's home, you will need to talk to that child outside of the home, so the school is the logical place to do that.

Some states are considering legislation that would require school officials to advise parents of an on-campus police interview. The exception normally built into these laws is that NO notification is to be made if the suspect is a family member.

There are occasions when there has been a disclosure of a molestation late in the afternoon and the child is sent home prior to Social Services and/or the police arriving at school. If the information is that the child is being molested at home, often it is better to wait until the next day when the child is back at school to interview them. Although this does set up a situation where the child could be victimized again prior to your interview, the odds of you obtaining the information that you need to protect the child for the long term is better if you wait until the following day.

If the molestation interview is conducted at school, follow the same formula/protocol as indicated earlier in this chapter.

CROSS-REPORTING TO THE CHILD ABUSE REGISTRY

California State law requires that you, as a mandated reporter of child abuse, contact the Child Abuse Registry by phone as soon as possible once you have learned of a child being sexually molested, physically abused, emotionally abused, or neglected. As soon as you have an opportunity to get to a telephone, you should call the Child Abuse Registry and supply them with the basic information they ask you over the phone. The person answering the phone will obtain the child's name, address, date of birth, the parents' information, and a brief synopsis as to what occurred. The social worker will also want to know if there is a need for an immediate response by the Social Services to come to meet you or if the child is going to be taken into protective custody.

The law requires that within thirty-six hours of this telephone report, the police reports and the appropriate forms for Social Services be mailed to the Child Abuse Registry. (See your individual state laws for reporting requirements.) Normally, this forwarding of the police reports is left to Detective personnel and/or Records personnel. Child Abuse Registries may accept a faxed copy in lieu of a mailed copy, but I encourage you to keep a copy of your transmission report. Additionally, some jurisdictions have made it a practice to document the name of the person at Social Services that took the telephone report. That's not a bad idea! Various states and counties have similar protective networks in place.

PHOTOGRAPHS AS EVIDENCE

During the course of your interview with the child, you should ask the child if any photographs were taken of him/her during the course of the molestation. You would also want to ask the child if any photographs of nude children or nude adults engaged in sexual acts were shown to them by the suspect prior to or during the course of that child's victimization. Obviously, this would be important information to know so that these photos can be seized, usually during the service of a search warrant.

Sample Report Narrative: 2-7 Year Old Victim

On 09-15-97 at 1500 hours, I met with victim 97-123 (Sarah) and her mother at home regarding a radio call report that Sarah was being molested during her weekend visitations at her father's home in Orange County. Sarah's mother told me that the suspect in this case was Sarah's biological father's roommate, Bill Smith. Sara's mother also provided identifying information on the suspect.

I interviewed Sarah while seated at the dining table inside the family home. After establishing rapport with her, I asked her if she could help me draw a stick figure of a girl. With Sarah's help, I completed a stick figure drawing, during which time we identified body parts, including her vaginal area, which she refers to as her "butterfly." Sara was also able to distinguish between "bad" and "good" touching.

I asked Sarah if anyone had ever touched her vaginal area in a "bad way." Sarah told me that someone had. She identified this person as being "Bill," adding that "Bill" is someone who lives with her father. She told me that every time she goes to visit with her father, "Bill" touches her on her vaginal area.

Sarah continued to state that this touching consisted of "Bill" using his hand to touch her on her vagina. She indicated that this happened in a skin-to-skin fashion, since he would remove her clothing just prior to touching her. I then used my index and middle fingers on my left hand to represent Sarah's vagina, and the index finger on my right hand to represent the suspect's finger. Rubbing the index finger of my right hand on the other two fingers, I asked Sarah if the touching occurred on the outside of her vagina, or if it occurred with the suspect putting his fingers inside her vagina. Sarah stated that the suspect put his fingers inside her vagina and indicated that he only put it in "a little bit." She did this by showing me, with her index finger, that he only penetrated the vagina perhaps one-half inch, or so, with his finger.

I asked Sarah if "Bill" had his clothes on or off at the time he was touching her. She told me that he would pull his "wiener" out of his pants as he was touching her. I used the same stick figure to identify his "wiener" as being his penis. Sarah went on to state that his penis was "sticking out straight" at the time that she saw it.

I asked Sarah if she touched "Bill's" penis during this time. She said that she did. I then used my ball point pen to represent the suspect's penis and asked Sarah to show me how she touched it. Sarah told me that the suspect took her hand and placed it on his penis, and while his hand was on top of hers, he moved her hand in an up-and-down motion on his penis. She demonstrated this to me using the ball point pen. I asked Sarah if anything came out of the suspect's penis while doing this, and she stated that the "white sticky stuff" came out.

I then asked Sarah if she could give me an approximation as to how big the suspect's penis was. I did this by using my two index fingers to represent a general length. Sarah, using her index fingers, showed me her representation of how long the suspect's penis was. I then had her place both of her index fingers down onto a piece of paper and I drew a line between the two index fingers. I later measured this distance and found it to be 6" long.

I asked Sarah if she could draw the suspect's penis for me, and she said she could. On the back of the piece of paper that the stick figure was drawn on, she drew me her representation of the suspect's penis. She identified his "wiener" and also drew what she referred to as "balls."

Sarah went on to state that the molesting took place in the suspect's bedroom. She told me that the suspect would take her in the bedroom, assist her in taking off her clothes, and then he would touch her in a skin-to-skin fashion with his hand. Sarah said that her father was out of the home when this took place, and she believed he was at the store or at work at the time the sexual touching took place.

Sarah went on to tell me that the touching took place on top of the suspect's bed and that he had a red blanket or bedspread on it. She added that the suspect told her this was a "secret game" that they were playing and that she should not tell anyone about it. The suspect also told her that if she told anyone about the game, that she (Sarah) might get into trouble.

I asked Sarah how many times this type of touching took place. She held up five fingers, saying it happened "that many times." At this point, Sarah's mother, who was present during the interview, indicated that she has been separated from her husband for the past six months, and that Sarah goes and visits him every weekend. She stated that about three months ago, the suspect, "Bill," became a full-time roommate at the father's home.

During the course of the interview, I also questioned Sarah as to whether or not she knew the difference between the truth and a lie. I noted that she was wearing a blue shirt. I pointed to her shirt and asked her what color it was. She correctly answered by saying it was blue. I asked her that if I were to say that the shirt was red instead of blue, would that be the truth or would it be a lie? She told me that that would be a lie. I then asked her if she was supposed to tell the truth or supposed to lie. She said that you are always supposed to tell the truth. I asked her what happens if she does not tell the truth, and she said that Mommy puts her in time-out if she lies.

Sarah said that no pictures were taken of her, nor was she shown pictures of other people. She also told me that the suspect only touched her vaginal area with his hand, as opposed to any other part of his body.

Due to the nature of the molestation as described by Sarah, I did not make arrangements for a medical examination to be conducted at this time. I did call the Child Abuse Registry and spoke with the on-duty worker, James Bullwinkle, and made a telephone report of the molestation incident to him. Sarah was not taken into protective custody at this time. I advised her mother not to allow any further visitations at the father's home until the police investigation could be completed.

INTERVIEW CHECKLIST

STICK FIGURE SYSTEM

CAUTION: Be sure to read and understand the Stick Figure System text before attempting to use this outline.

- ✓ High Five/How old are you?/You're big for your age
- ✓ Sit at corner of table
- ✓ Trace hands
- ✓ Draw a PEOPLE
- ✓ Identify body parts
- ✓ If you don't know the answer, it's OK
- ✓ Is it OK for people to touch you on_____?
- ✓ Did anyone touch you on_____(genitals)?
- ✓ Who touched you, with what?
- ✓ Playing a game vs. being mean
- ✓ Demo inside vs outside touching
- ✓ Break—-Truth vs. lies
- ✓ Suspects clothes; on / off
- ✓ Penis; erect/non-erect
- ✓ Draw size-length of penis (optional)
- ✓ Good vs. bad touch
- ✓ Secrets (optional)
- ✓ Break—-Family members, ages etc.
- ✓ Associated details: day/night, what room, others present, additional victims, photos, etc.

Attention span varies with maturity... use breaks accordingly.

(Fig. 11 Interview Checklist)

Chapter 3

INTERVIEWING CHILDREN AGES 8-12

Eight to twelve-year-olds are obviously more verbal than the younger children, so there is no need to go through as extensive a rapport establishing process. However, it is important to develop a friendly non-threatening relationship before beginning the interview.

BACKGROUND

As before, a brief overview is all that is needed. Therefore not contaminating any statement from the child.

SEATING ARRANGEMENT

The seating arrangement with the child should be the same, although you might not want to sit quite as close to them and you don't want them crawling in your lap toward the end of the interview. Also, there is no need to trace hands or to draw a stick figure with a child of this age to identify body parts. However, it is necessary to identify some general terms with them.

TERMINOLOGY

Since, as I have discussed, an officer may testify at the preliminary hearing for the child, you will have to establish that you did clarify the terms used in your report with the child. A child merely telling you that they had "sex" with the suspect is not sufficient. You will have to identify that "sex" means "sexual intercourse," and that this term means the suspect placed his penis into the vagina of the child. You will also have to establish a definition for "oral copulation," "sodomy," or any other terms you've used in your report that the child might have disclosed to you in their language.

TEAMING WITH SOCIAL SERVICES

If the child is disclosing an in-family molestation situation, it is quite likely that this information will come forward at school. You might want to consider "teaming" with Social Services so that the protective custody issues can be dealt with at the same time that the criminal investigation/interview is done.

OUT-OF-HOME SUSPECT

It is quite possible that the child is going to disclose an ongoing molestation situation with multiple sexual acts over an extended period of time. This is because a child of this age is out of the view of the parents for a greater length of time, either going to school or going to Little League practice, Scouts, or other activities away from home. These children are also being watched in after-school day care situations. It is also possible that the child has been targeted by a stepparent who has entered the family with the specific purpose of having sex with the child. You should be prepared to conduct a rather lengthy interview with this child, because they will be disclosing to you multiple acts which occurred over an extended length of time.

VICTIM / SUSPECT PROFILE

Long-term molestation situations may go undetected for a long time. This is often due to the profile of the victim and the manipulative nature of the predator. Statistically, a child victim of long-term molestation criminal activity will be one who is feeling neglected at home and not having his or her emotional needs or concerns met. As a result, the child tends to seek out someone who *will* pay attention. Unfortunately, many times they will find a child molester to give them the emotional pat on the back they seek. In exchange for that positive input from the adult, the child has to allow the sexual touching.

As stated before, there are several types of sexual offenders and I encourage you to read several of the books listed in the bibliography that discuss, in detail, the profile of sexual predators. Nicholas Groth (*Sexual Assault of Adolescents and Children*) states in his book, and I strongly agree with him, that in order to understand the crime, you must understand the criminal. Suffice it to say, for this textbook purpose, sexual predators come in all shapes and sizes, may be either sex, exist in all ethnic and educational levels and can be found as often in a church as in a farm environment. They may be boy scout leaders, priests, construction workers, ministers, teachers or police officers. Only two of the most common offenders will be discussed in any detail in the subsequent text for purposes of better investigation reports and to provide the investigator enough information to adequately ask the right questions.

The common factor with all offenders is that they *seek out vulnerable children from whom they receive their emotional and sexual gratification.*

VICTIM GENDER

My experience has been that there are an equal number of male and female victims. This means that a suspect may molest both males and females, or he may exclusively molest one or the other sex. If you are dealing with an in-family molestation situation where one of the girls has come forward to talk about a molestation allegation, you obviously have to talk to all of the girls in the home. You also have to talk to the boys. Sex offenders have a tendency to see children as a non-sexual group unto themselves. This means that they do not see the children as being boy children and girl children; they simply see them as one group, as "children." For this reason, they are equally vulnerable, and both sexes have to be interviewed once there has been a disclosure of a molestation within a family.

FAMILY DYNAMICS

Since victims are more verbal at this age, they should be able to give you a lot of detail about the dynamics of the family situation and of the relationship between themselves and the suspect. This is very important information for the person who is going to interview the suspect later on.

NUMBER OF COUNTS

A child of this age will be able to detail with some accuracy the number of times there has been sexual contact between the child and the adult. Generally, you first ask the child when the last time any sexual contact took place. This will normally be a few days, or perhaps a week or two prior to your interview. Then you would ask the child when their very first time was. The child is normally able to recall a general time frame as to when the very first sexual act took place. You then try to tie down other time frames by asking, "Do you recall a time when there was a molestation during Christmas vacation or perhaps Easter, the end of the school year, during the summer, between the 4th and 5th grades, or right at the time school started, at Halloween, or Thanksgiving?"

It is not sufficient just to say that there were "about a hundred sexual contacts between the suspect and the child." What you should try to do is tie down each incident that the child can remember, within a time frame, as a specific crime detailing what actually took place at that time. This allows the District Attorney to file multiple counts against the suspect during those time frames.

ATTENTION SPAN

With a child of this age, there is not as much need to be as concerned about them becoming fatigued or being unable to pay attention to the interviewer over an extended length of time. However, if the interview is going to be very lengthy, you might want to take a break for a few minutes and get up and walk around with the child, or talk about something else for a couple of minutes just to give you and the child a little time to relax from the tension of the interview.

QUALIFYING AS A WITNESS

A child of this age normally does not need to be qualified as a witness. It is assumed that someone this age already knows the difference between telling the truth and telling a lie. However, if the child has some sort of disability or handicap or mental problem that you think might allow the issue to be raised in court, then you should go ahead and qualify the child as a witness as you would do with a much younger child.

DISCUSSION

When you receive a call that is going to put you in contact with a child of this age range, you will have to assume that you are going to be involved in a rather lengthy interview process. Assume at least a forty-five minute interview with the child.

Even if the child is being molested by someone outside of his family, such as a neighbor, coach or scout leader, you may have to take the child into protective custody, depending on the parents' ability to protect the child and keep him away from the offender. Often, these children are "throw away" children. The parents may not be terribly protective of the child once the molestation has been disclosed. It is this lack of concern on the part of the parent that has led to the molestation.

Although you will not have to identify body parts in the same fashion as you do with younger children, you should not overlook the possibility that the older child can give you more description as to what the suspect's body actually looks like. If there are scars, tattoos, birthmarks, or deformities that the child has witnessed, you should solicit this information from the child, since it is very important corroborative evidence to the molestation allegation. You should also question the child as to whether or not he or she has been photographed by the suspect, when the last time they saw these photographs, and where the photographs are kept. This will allow a search warrant to be prepared to look for those evidentiary items.

CROSS-REPORTING

This type of molestation situation has to be cross-reported to the Child Abuse Registry, just like any other allegation of child abuse. If the child is being victimized by someone inside their family, Social Services will normally respond within two hours to help make a determination as to whether or not the child should be taken into protective custody. If the child is being victimized by an out-of-family perpetrator, frequently, they will respond within ten days, as opposed to immediately.

NUMBER OF COUNTS

It is not unusual for a child in this age range to only tell you about 25% of the actual times there was sexual contact between them and the adult. There is a tendency to downplay the severity of the molestation, either by reducing the number of times there was sexual contact, or minimizing the sexual contact to fondling, when there was actual intercourse or oral sex. It is important that you tell the child that you need to know all of what took place so that you can get a complete picture of what was actually transpiring. If you fail to *get it all*, you may be faced with additional allegations surfacing during court testimony.

When the child testifies in court to a different set of molestation incidents than they told you about, a problem exists. The child is not lying; he is simply telling the other 75% of what actually took place. As a result, *if you did not get it all, get it right* and *get it all the first time,* it makes the child look as if he were lying in court. It is important to explain this to the child so they will feel more comfortable in telling you as much as they can actually recall during that initial interview.

When you write the police report, make an allowance for the other 75% of the story. You do this by giving a general overview of the molestation in the first part of your report. An example of this would be, "The victim said that he had sex with the suspect three times a week for the last six months." If the victim can only detail one or two of these actual molestations during that time frame, you then become more specific about those incidents that they can specifically recall. This way, in court, when the victim recalls more specific incidents than he did during your interview, it doesn't make it look like they are lying.

FALSE REPORTS

False reports by children in this age range are relatively rare, because they are not as easily influenced by adults as younger children are. However they are keenly aware of any friction between estranged parents. Occasionally, they will try to appease one parent by saying that they don't like to visit the other parent or that something "bad" happened during the last visit. This "bad thing" can be twisted into a molest allegation, followed by an attempt to end or change custody and/or visitation. The child is now stuck with a "story" that he/she cannot recant.

INTERVIEW: 8-12 YEAR-OLD VICTIM

The officer receives a call to meet with a social worker at a grammar school regarding the possible molestation of a nine-year-old boy. Upon arrival, the officer should meet with the social worker and obtain a general overview of the allegations. In this way, the interview will not be contaminated. You should tell the school officials to *NOT CALL THE PARENTS* because of the possibility that they might be suspects and/or the officer may have to take the child into protective custody. You don't want to find yourself in a situation where an angry parent bursts into the middle of your interview telling the kid to "*Shut Up*" before you have established the elements of a crime.

Find a private room in which to conduct the interview. I prefer to use a conference room because it generally has a larger table. This enables me to use the preferred table corner seating arrangement, allowing me to sit at 90° to the child. By using the conference or meeting room rather than an office, there is less chance you will be interrupted by a phone ringing or someone's need to "interrupt for just a moment" to obtain papers from their desk.

At first you don't sit too close to the child and ask a few introductory questions about his family, school and outside activities in order to establish rapport and get an idea of his or her language level and maturity. Tell the child that the social worker has told you about the molestation allegations but that you need more information so that the child can help you figure out what happened and what to do next. When you start to ask about the molestation, move closer to the child and let him see that you are taking notes which indicates you are interested in what he has to say. The written notes, however, should be very brief so that the silence while you write does not cause long pauses in the conversation.

I usually start by asking the child how he first met the suspect, and when the sexual touching first started. I then tell the child, "I need to be sure that I understand you." which leads you into a conversation to define terms for genitals and the sexual acts. I then get a general overview of the allegations and tie down more specifics/time frames. I always close the conversation by asking the child if they have any questions of me.

Sample Report Narrative: 8-12 Year Old Victim

On 8-23-96, at 1130 hours, I went to Sunnyvale School and met with Social Worker Randy Snodgrass. Snodgrass told me that he had been called to the school by the school nurse regarding the disclosure of an ongoing sexual molestation of a nine-year-old boy, Victim #96-102 (Ryan).

Ryan had disclosed to the school nurse that after school each day, he was being baby-sat by a neighbor who had routinely been having sexual contact with him. Apparently, Ryan had disclosed the molestation to his family several weeks ago and they responded by telling Ryan to simply "stay away from him," but continued to allow him to go over to the suspect's residence. I then had Ryan brought into the room, where Social Worker Snodgrass and I spoke to him. I found Ryan to be a bright and articulate nine-year old whose mannerisms were age appropriate.

By way of background information, Ryan told me that approximately a year ago, his mother started to work a full-time job during the day. Arrangements were made for him to go to a neighbor's house after school. The neighbor had volunteered free after-school day care for Ryan between about 3:00 p.m. and 6:00 p.m. Ryan identified the suspect, as indicated on the face page, as a male, white, in his mid 30's.

Ryan went on to state that initially, his contacts with the suspect consisted of the suspect helping Ryan with his homework and playing video games. As time went on, the suspect began to have Ryan sit on his lap as they played video games. The suspect began to rub the inside of Ryan's thighs over his clothing and ultimately began touching Ryan's genitals over his clothing. Ryan stated that he had been at the suspect's residence for approximately one month before the actual touching of his genitals took place.

Ryan told me that as the sexual touching progressed, both he and the suspect would take their clothes off in both the living room and sometimes in the bedroom of the suspect's home. They would then engage in mutual oral sex and masturbation of each other. Ryan indicated that initially, the suspect stated he wanted to teach Ryan "how to masturbate." The suspect would disrobe in front of Ryan and masturbate his own penis until he ejaculated. The suspect would then undress Ryan and then masturbate him in a similar fashion. As the relationship continued, the suspect convinced Ryan that he (Ryan) should masturbate the suspect's penis while, at the same time, the suspect masturbated Ryan.

Ryan continued, that about two months ago, the sexual relationship escalated to where the suspect began performing oral sex on Ryan. Ryan stated that there were approximately ten times where the suspect performed oral sex on Ryan's penis. Ryan went on to state that about two weeks ago, the suspect asked Ryan to perform oral sex on him. Ryan did, in fact, put his mouth on the suspect's penis on three different occasions within the last two weeks.

Ryan stated that the last time there was any sexual activity between him and the suspect was last Friday. He said that during that particular incident, he went to the suspect's house after school and the suspect invited him into the his bedroom. At that time, both Ryan and the suspect disrobed and the suspect orally copulated Ryan's penis for perhaps ten minutes. The suspect then sat down on the bed, removed his own pants, and asked Ryan to orally copulate him. Ryan orally copulated the suspect's penis for two or three minutes and then masturbated the suspect until he ejaculated.

Ryan estimated that the first time there was any actual sexual contact between him and the suspect would have been about a month and a half to two months after the start of the school year of 1995. He stated that the sexual acts then continued three or four times a week, every week, for the next year or so.

Ryan specifically recalls that on the Friday after Thanksgiving of 1995, he was going to spend the entire day at the suspect's residence, since both of his parents were going to be out of town. On this particular day, Ryan stated that while playing video games in the suspect's living room, the suspect masturbated Ryan twice and had Ryan masturbate the suspect on two separate occasions.

Ryan also stated that during Christmas break of 1995, there were numerous times when he had sexual contact with the suspect. Ryan specifically recalls one incident that occurred in the evening hours at the suspect's residence. He stated that he had had dinner at the suspect's house that night and, after dinner, the suspect took him into the bedroom. At this time, the suspect removed Ryan's pants, orally copulated him while inserting one finger into Ryan's rectum. After the suspect orally copulated Ryan for about five minutes, Ryan masturbated the suspect until he ejaculated.

Ryan went on to state that on his birthday, in March of 1996, the suspect took him out to a movie. On the way home from the movie, the suspect parked his vehicle in a closed commercial area, approximately one-half mile away from Ryan's home. While in this darkened commercial area, the suspect orally copulated Ryan's penis and Ryan then masturbated the suspect until he ejaculated.

Ryan indicated that his sexual contacts with the suspect continued on a weekly basis throughout the remainder of the school year and throughout the first month or so of the summer of 1996. Ryan stated that he became increasingly uncomfortable with the sexual contact by the suspect and that the suspect wanted more oral sex from Ryan.

Ryan stated that he finally told his parents about the sexual victimization. He stated that his parents did not seem overly concerned about this and simply told him to refuse any further sexual contacts with the suspect. They told him to continue going to the suspect's house for after-school day care purposes, but to simply refuse any further sexual contact with him. Ryan stated that he attempted to refuse the sexual advances by the suspect after that time; however, they continued and became more severe since Ryan now began performing oral sex on the suspect.

Ryan also indicated that several times during his relationship with the suspect, the suspect showed him commercially produced photographs of nude adults in magazines. These adults were engaged in both vaginal and anal intercourse, along with oral sex. The pictures included both heterosexual and homosexual activity. Ryan added that about six months ago, the suspect did convince him to pose nude for some Polaroid-type photographs. Ryan stated that these photographs are kept in a shoe box underneath the suspect's bed in his residence. The last time Ryan saw these photographs was about three months ago.

Nothing further was gained from the interview with Ryan. It was decided by the social worker and me that he should be taken into protective custody since it did not appear that his parents were willing to protect him from the suspect. Ryan does not have any siblings and he was unaware of any other children who were being molested by the suspect at this time.

Chapter 4

INTERVIEWING AGES 13-18

BACKGROUND INFORMATION

This generally tends to be more sketchy than with the younger children due to reluctance on the part of the victim to openly disclose details of the molestation to anybody. The victims tend to understand the sexual and social nature of the offense and society's general phobia about sexual acts in general. As a result, they are a little more reluctant to be open about what has taken place.

If the child has been involved in a long-term sexual relationship with the suspect, there is a great possibility that they will have some *positive* feelings about the offender. They will also have some guilt feelings about divulging the relationship and their participation in it. These long-term relationships involve a coercion into the sexual activity by a non-complaining victim, as opposed to the forced sexual victimization in a one-time rape-type scenario.

For this reason, you again run into a situation in which the child is normally willing to talk about 25-30% of the actual numbers of sexual acts. As previously stated, this creates a problem in court when, as the child is more comfortable later in revealing more of what took place, they talk about added sexual encounters that they did not give the initial officer.

FIRST CONTACT WITH THE VICTIM

These children are old enough to understand why you are there and that you have been called to the scene to interview them with regards to the molestation situation. Introducing yourself by name and explaining the purpose of your visit is normally all of the introduction you need with children in this age range. Children of this age span are often fearful, suspicious or even have a dislike of law enforcement, so some friendly discussion of a general nature may help to establish a degree of rapport which will enable you to begin the interview.

BUILDING RAPPORT WITH A TEEN

The simplest way to develop rapport with a teenage molestation victim is to treat them "like a real person." This may sound like an oversimplification, but if you approach them in a business-like manner and talk to them like young adults, you will accomplish your goal of gathering as much information as possible.

These teens have been treated like sex "objects" for a large part of their lives. They've been lied to, manipulated, used and thrown away. What they don't want is for some officer to be condescending, aloof, arrogant, indignant or judgmental. Don't pat them on the head and tell them to be a "nice little girl" or tell them "tell me what happened and I'll make it better." Talking down to them like that is a form of manipulation that they'll see right through and probably decide not to talk to you.

Also, do not try to win them over by telling them how angry or disgusted you are with someone who would "do something like that" to a child. That type of statement is a double-edged sword that cuts two ways, both bad. First, the victim may have some positive feelings for the suspect. If so, you've just thrown up another hurdle between you and the child. Secondly, those "disgusting acts" are something that she or he has been doing for a long time. As a result, the child will assume that you are angry and disgusted at them too and see them as something less than human.

The point is that the teenage molestation victim will not be able to make the subtle distinction between your disgust for the suspect and your feelings toward them.

MANIPULATION BY VICTIMS

Some of the victims who have been involved in long-term relationships, especially in an in-family type situation, have learned to be very manipulative of adults and of their environment. If that has been the case with the child you are dealing with, they will also attempt to manipulate you during the course of the interview.

With that in mind, you have to put on your "no nonsense face." This means that you have to take charge of the situation without being overbearing. You have to let the child know that you have a legitimate reason for knowing the intimate details of what took place and that you are not going to accept anything less than that.

These children have learned that they can frequently avoid any scrutiny by adults by simply smiling or giving a passive type of answer without any great detail. Let the child know by your demeanor that you are not going to allow that to happen. You also have to let them know that you have heard "everything" before and you are not going to be embarrassed by what the child has to say, nor are you going to be critical of their involvement in an ongoing sexual relationship.

You can also tell the child that since you are familiar with all of the "street language" that they might know, it is okay for them to use that type of terminology. However, once again, you might want to identify terms just to be absolutely certain that you are talking about the same things. Once you have identified their common terms for actual sexual acts, you should use the more clinical terms for the remainder of your report. Also, if you begin to use the clinical terms during the course of your interview (e.g., intercourse versus "screw"), the victim has a tendency to begin using those terms also. This helps the victim distance themselves from the actual emotional impact of the events and it prepares them for courtroom testimony.

Sample Report Narrative: Manipulative Teenage Victim

On 10-16-97, at 0930 hours, I met with victim 97-125, Jennifer, a fourteen-year-old female, and her mother, Mrs. Carlson, at their home. Mrs. Carlson stated that she was concerned that her daughter was sexually active with Mrs. Carlson's second husband (Jennifer's stepfather, identified as the suspect).

Mrs. Carlson stated she became suspicious last week when she received a telephone call from Jennifer's school. Apparently, Jennifer had not been attending class for the last several weeks. Mrs. Carlson was totally unaware of this. She stated that it was a normal routine for the suspect to take Jennifer to school on his way to work. When Mrs. Carlson learned that the suspect had been calling the school and indicating that Jennifer was sick each day, she felt something was going on.

Mrs. Carlson went on to explain that over the last several months, she has become concerned about the closeness of the relationship between Jennifer and the suspect. She stated it is not unusual for them to hold hands when they are out in public together and he seems to be addressing her more like a girlfriend rather than a stepdaughter.

I questioned Mrs. Carlson about her relationship with the suspect. She told me that they have been married for the last four years. She married him shortly after her divorce from a very abusive first husband, Jennifer's biological father. Since the divorce, she has not had any contact with Jennifer's biological father, nor has he had any contact with Jennifer. Mrs. Carlson stated that when she married the suspect, it was more a marriage of convenience rather than of love. She stated that her sexual activity with the suspect is very infrequent. She stated she married him more because he was very nice to Jennifer and he made very few demands of her, either sexually or otherwise. Mrs. Carlson saw this as a welcome relief from the relationship she had with her abusive first husband.

Mrs. Carlson went on to say that in the last six to eight months, it had not been unusual for the suspect to come to the breakfast table wearing female clothing. She stated that he would often explain that it was because she was "frigid" and that he needed to wear this apparel to relieve his sexual needs. She also saw him masturbating frequently while wearing women's clothing.

Mrs. Carlson stated that when she realized that Jennifer was not going to school, she feared that perhaps there was more going on between the suspect and Jennifer. With that in mind, she began to search through the suspect's belongings and in his closet. She found a locked briefcase which she forced open and found approximately one hundred (100) photographs inside. Many of the photographs were of Jennifer posing nude, and some were of Jennifer involved in sexual activity with the suspect.

Mrs. Carlson stated that last night, she had confronted her husband with the photographs. He became very angry at her, telling her that she had no business prying into his personal property. The suspect then collected many of his personal belongings, including the briefcase with the photos inside, and moved out of the home. Mrs. Carlson stated that she had kept a half dozen of the photographs and had them in her purse. She gave them to me for evidence purposes. I saw that these photographs were sexually explicit since they showed Jennifer involved in both oral and vaginal sex with the suspect.

Mrs. Carlson added that Jennifer has refused to talk to her about this problem and has denied any sexual involvement with the suspect even when confronted with the photographs.

I then had Jennifer join her mother and me at the dining table where I tried to question her about the sexual relationship. Jennifer was uncooperative and stated she did not want to talk about what had taken place. She told me that it was her business and none of mine. She stated that she did not feel that she had been victimized at all, and that she was not going to assist in any sort of criminal prosecution or investigation involving the suspect.

I talked with Jennifer for several minutes before she decided to finally disclose some of the sexual involvement between her and the suspect. She would only discuss the sexual activity that was depicted in the six photographs which her mother still had in her possession. Jennifer did identify herself and the suspect as being the people involved in the photographs and that they were taken inside the family home. She stated that the sexual acts "just happened," and she would not elaborate as to the relationship that led up to the photographs being taken or the number of times she was involved sexually with the suspect.

Jennifer stated that if anyone was to blame for the sexual acts, it was her mother, because had her mother been more sexually involved with the suspect, then Jennifer would not have had to substitute for the mother as a lover for the suspect.

Jennifer refused to give any further statement as to her involvement with the suspect. Mrs. Carlson added that she did not know the suspect's current whereabouts, but assumed he was staying in a motel in the general area.

MALE PERPETRATOR - MALE VICTIM

It is quite possible that there are more male victims of child molestation in this age range than female victims. There are a number of reasons that lead me to this opinion, but suffice it to say that there are a lot of male suspects engaging in a lot of sexual activity with underage boys. However, because of society's homosexual stigma to such activities, a lot of these crimes go unreported.

When you do come across such a case, you need to explain to the victim that the actual sexual victimization itself does not mean that they are a homosexual. You have to explain to them that their penis has a "head of its own" and, frequently, it enjoys the sexual contact without understanding the social implications of the male on male activity.

This is especially true of boys who have been victimized over a great length of time, with the molestations beginning when they were approximately 7-to-9-years-old and continuing on into their early teens. When the molestations initially started, they did not attach any sort of homosexual phobias to it, but as they grew older, they began to understand how society views such events. Unfortunately for these kids, once such a sexual relationship develops, it is very difficult for them to get out of that relationship.

Also, in these types of relationships the victim will often have some positive feelings toward the suspect. Many of these victims are seeking some sort of positive influence from an adult, something they are lacking in their home environment. When they find someone who is willing to pay them that positive attention, they frequently end up being victimized by that very person. Since they have no one else in their lives giving them positive input or enhanced self-esteem, they are often reluctant to give up the molester. As stated earlier, you need a combination of victim and suspect profiles for these long-term relationships to continue.

The victim in this type of case has a tendency to diminish the severity of the offense, either by vastly underestimating the number of sexual contacts between him and the suspect or diminishing the severity of them. Sometimes, the child will say they were only fondled, when they had actually been engaged in oral sex. Or, they will say the sexual contact occurred 10 or 20 times, when there were actually several hundred times.

It is also possible that a child in this relationship has been recruiting other children for the offender. Since this type of offender generally prefers children of a certain age range, he has to continually recruit children within that age category. For that reason, it is quite possible that the victim you are talking to was recruited by an older boy at one time and is now recruiting younger children to replace him when he becomes too old for the offender. You need to ask the child about this possibility since you might be able to identify additional victims.

The FBI refers to this as a "pipeline theory." Basically, at one end of the pipeline, you have the offender, who is attracting/recruiting potential victims to him. Normally, this is someone who puts himself in the position to have contact with lots of potential victims, such as a Boy Scout leader or video game arcade operator. As he identifies potential victims, he draws them into the "pipeline," during which time the molestation takes place. During the course of several months or years, the molesting continues until the child becomes too old and, in essence, is deposited on the opposite side of the "pipeline" and discarded because he is no longer sexually attractive to the offender.

Many potential victims are attracted to the offender. Only a few are molested, then discarded.

(Fig. 12) FBI's Pipeline Theory

MALE PERPETRATOR - FEMALE VICTIM

These can be short term or long term relationships with varying dynamics. As you'll see in future chapters in the short term relationships the suspect will see the victim as the sexual aggressor, somehow being "older" than their actual age. This is true in both in-family and out-of-family perpetrators.

In longer term relationships the victim can develop a variety of feelings for the suspect, from caring and protective to fear and hate. Her overwhelming fear maybe her families reaction to the telling of her secret.

INCEST

The law requires that there be actual vaginal intercourse to complete the element of the crime, along with a blood relationship between the suspect and victim. However, the dynamics of the incestuous family, in a clinical sense, would include step-father/daughter relationships, and also sexual acts that only involve oral sex, or sodomy, or fondling.

What happens in an in-family situation like this is that there is a shift in the family structure from what is considered "normal." Basically, there is a realignment of the family structure in which the father becomes closely aligned to the children and the mother is, in essence, an absentee parent. With the absence of the mother as an active participant in the family, a vacuum of sorts is created between the father and the children, which allows them to closely align to each other.

If the father is so inclined to be a child molester, he then will target the children, who are now very vulnerable and accessible to him. The same dynamics can occur with the female/mother as the suspect, but reporting of such incidents is much rarer than the father being the suspect. In such families, both male and female children can be victimized. (Refer to the following illustration)

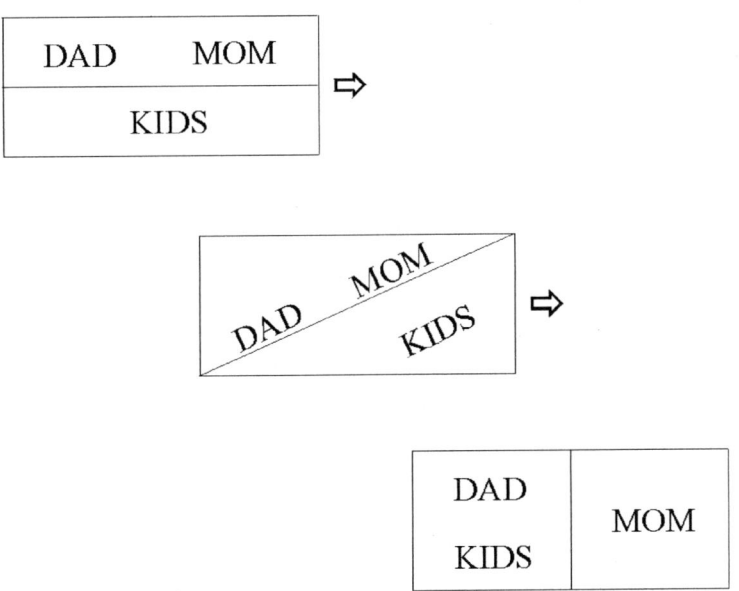

(Fig. 13) Shift in family structure that leads to incest

In this type of family structure, the child has learned that sex, self-esteem and power are all rolled up together. Because of this, they can be very manipulative within the family and will attempt to manipulate your interview. Sometimes, they won't want to give up the position of power that they have within the family structure, and will downplay the number of times they were involved sexually with the parent.

Occasionally you will find a family structure in which the suspect is clinically a rapist, as opposed to a child molester or someone whose sexual preference is actually for children. In this type of situation, the dynamics of the family are dramatically different from that described above. In this type of situation, you will not see a dating-type relationship in which the child is now seen as an age mate to the adult/suspect. The sexual events are more forced and demanded as opposed to coerced and cajoled. The mother is still a non-functioning parent within the home and has frequently been so berated by the father that she either fails to see or refuses to see the sexual victimization of her own child.

In this family situation, the child does not have any power within the family structure itself. The child is taught that they have no control over what happens to their body. The child has to submit to the sexual demands of the parent. This causes problems later on in life when this child is now in a dating situation and does not feel powerful enough to say no to the sexual advances of their age mates. This can result in a lot of date rape type scenarios in which the victim did not want to have sex with her date, but she never actively said "no" either.

A family structure with an "in-family rapist" results in a victim with very low self-esteem and a complete blocking of emotions concerning the sexual acts themselves. During an interview of such a child, there may be a complete flat affect with respect to the way she responds to questions about the sexual acts themselves. She may be very "matter-of-fact" about what actually took place. This type of child is not as manipulative as the other in-family victim, since she has not been given any sort of power or pay-back for being involved sexually with the parent. This is also the type of child who will be trying to escape the family environment and will have a history of running away, of committing petty crimes, and other activities that might keep her away from the home.

This type of child basically distrusts all authority figures. She has learned that the parents, who are supposed to protect you in life, actually take advantage of you, so she is not about to trust a stranger to protect her.

In incest and family rape, you have to question the child about sexually explicit photographs being taken of them or shown to them. You also need to ask about any sort of sexual toys or devices that are used during the sexual acts. All of these items are potential evidence to be seized under a search warrant.

Sample Report Narrative: Incest Victim

On 2/02/98, at 0700 hours, I arrived at work. I was contacted by patrol officers, who were speaking with victim #98-020 (Barbara), a 15-year-old female. Patrol personnel told me that they had come into contact with Barbara early this morning. They found her walking down Main Street at about 4:00 a.m. She was visibly upset about something. She told patrol officers that she had run away because her biological father, the suspect, had been molesting her. Patrol officers then brought Barbara to the police department and obtained some basic information from her about the molestation allegation. Patrol requested that I conduct the in-depth interview with her.

I was introduced to Barbara in the Detective Bureau lobby. I took her to the cafeteria area located in the basement of the City Hall building across the courtyard from the police department. At this time of day, the dining area of the cafeteria was empty and I chose to talk with her at a corner table in the cafeteria.

I told Barbara that I was interested in obtaining as much detail as I could about the molestation allegation and that I needed to know this information for various legal reasons. I also told her that the more facts I had, the more I would be able to do for her and help her to prevent this from happening to her again.

By way of background information, Barbara stated that she lives at home with her father, the suspect, and her eight-year-old brother. She said that about four years ago, her mother and father separated and that her alcoholic mother moved out of the home. Barbara has had very limited contact with the mother since that time.

Barbara told me that on her 13th birthday she first had a sexual contact with her father. She told me that on that day, he called her into his bedroom in the early evening hours. He told her that she was old enough to "learn about sex." He told her that he was going to teach her things that she would need to know when she got married. Initially, her father disrobed in front of her and exposed his genitals to her. He then told her that he wanted her to touch his genitals so she would know "what a man feels like." She stated that when she did this, her father's penis became erect. She told me that she was frightened by what was happening, but she did not know what to do to prevent it.

The suspect then told Barbara that she should disrobe in front of him. She told me that she took off all of her clothing except for her panties and bra. At that point, the suspect began to fondle her breasts, telling her that eventually, she would learn to like that type of touching and this was the type of touching that her boyfriends and husband would ultimately do to her. Nothing else happened that night.

Barbara said that two weeks later, her father again called her into his bedroom. At that time, he told her to completely disrobe and he began to fondle her breasts and vaginal area in a skin-to-skin fashion and ultimately masturbated in front of her. He told her it was necessary for her to learn "what happens" during sex, and that is why he masturbated in front of her.

Barbara stated that it was exactly two weeks later when the suspect called her into his bedroom, had her disrobe, and this time had vaginal intercourse with her. She stated that he wore a condom when he did this and told her that she needed to learn about "safe sex." He also told her that as long as he wore a condom, it wasn't like they were actually having intercourse and she would still be considered a virgin.

Barbara said that from that date forward, she had sexual contact with the suspect every other Wednesday night and that it was his routine. Barbara stated that there were *some* special days, however, when the suspect would deviate from the every other Wednesday night pattern. Those days were: the suspect's birthday, Christmas, New Year's and the Fourth of July.

She stated that the suspect told her it was easier for him to have sex with her as opposed to hiring a prostitute or engaging in a dating relationship with an adult female. He told her that it was simply easier for him to have the relationship with her, and it also taught her about sex. The suspect said that someday she would be thankful for his instruction in this area.

According to Barbara, the regular sexual activity has been consistent for the past two years. Because of that, she has run away from home several times over the last few months in an attempt to escape her father. However, each time she has gone back home because she did not know where else to go. She also told me that she did not think anyone would believe her if she were to tell them what was happening at home.

Barbara told me that she ran away the previous night rather than have sex with her father. She told me that she climbed out of her bedroom window shortly after dinner to escape from being called to his bedroom to have sex with him.

Barbara went on to state that every time she had vaginal intercourse with the suspect, he always wore a condom and that he kept a supply of condoms in the night stand near his bed.

Barbara also stated that several times he had shown her sexually explicit photographs from adult magazines. He would suggest that they engage in the type of sexual activity depicted on the magazine pages. Specifically, he was making reference to oral and anal sex. Barbara was reluctant to engage in these activities and the suspect never forced them on her. She stated that each time they had intercourse, she would just lie on her back on top of his bed and the intercourse would take perhaps two to three minutes.

I returned to the Detective Bureau with Barbara. I called Records and found out that the suspect had reported his daughter as a runaway last night. I also found three prior runaway reports on her.

I told Barbara I was interested in her making a clandestine telephone call to the suspect. I explained the nature of the call, that being that she should attempt to solicit statements from him that would amount to admissions to his sexual involvement with her. I told her she would have to be very specific to be sure that we were talking about a *sexual* relationship between her and the suspect, as opposed to any other type of relationship. I spent about fifteen minutes explaining the nature and procedure for the call, and Barbara stated she was willing to do so.

I went into the "cold room" inside the Narcotic Unit. The "cold room" is set up with a telephone where a conversation can be monitored and recorded. I called my own extension at the police department to test the equipment. I listed the case number, date and time of the call as well as the nature of it. (*NOTE*: You should always play the recording back to make sure your equipment is working and check your own state's laws regarding the recording of phone conversations.)

I then asked Barbara to join me in the "cold room." After I dialed the suspect's telephone number, I handed the phone to her, placing the headphones on my head so I could listen to both sides of the conversation while it was being taped.

When the suspect answered the phone, Barbara identified herself and stated that she was calling from a friend's house and that she only had a few minutes to talk. The suspect asked her why she had run away again, and she responded by stating she ran away because she did not want to have sex with him anymore. The call lasted approximately ten to fifteen minutes, during which the suspect repeatedly stated that the reason he was having sex with her was because it was better for the family that he do so, as opposed to him having a girlfriend that would take him away from the family.

During the call, she stated several times that she did not want to have sexual intercourse with him anymore, nor was she interested in engaging in other sexual acts that he continued to show her via the adult magazines. The suspect said that if she was really serious about not wanting to have sex with him, they could discuss it if she would return home. Barbara told him that she did not know if she was going to come home and, at my direction, she ended the call by hanging up on him.

I made arrangements for Barbara to be taken into protective custody and prepared a search warrant for the suspect's residence in order to obtain the condoms and the sexually explicit magazines described by Barbara.

FEMALE PERPETRATORS - FEMALE VICTIMS

This is probably the *least reported* type of sexual victimization. In the few cases I have handled, I have seen the same dynamics as in male suspects and female victims since the victim suffers the same loss of self-esteem, ability to trust and suffers from fear of reprisal or disapproval from the victimizer or from society. This type of victimization occurs to victims ranging from infancy through late teens. When interviewing the victim or suspect in this type of case, you simply need to understand the dynamics of the relationship, as in all cases, and your interview is the same as it would be where there is a male suspect and male victim. The same rules and techniques should be applied in both situations and as set out in the next paragraph.

FEMALE PERPETRATORS - MALE VICTIMS

Adult females having sex with underage males is a crime that is vastly under-reported. This is due to the duality in thinking (a double standard) in America that if a female is a victim of a sexual assault, it needs to be reported and someone needs to be prosecuted, but if an adult female has sex with a young boy, it is unfortunately considered by most to be a passage into manhood.

Because of this double standard, many of these types of crimes do not get reported. Frequently, society sees a teenage boy who is having sex with an adult female as being "lucky," and that this type of relationship is his passage into manhood. Some states' laws are very clear that such relationships are criminal in the same sense as if the sexes were reversed. For example, in recent years, California made the law of "Unlawful Intercourse With a Person Under Age 18 Years," gender neutral. (See your individual state laws.)

When interviewing such a male victim, you should do so in the same fashion as you would a female victim.

The "Mrs. Robinson Syndrome" has been romanticized in our culture. *Summer of '42* and *Private Lessons* are other film examples of glorifying the exploitation of a young male by an adult female. However, the traumatic effect on a victim of such a crime can be devastating and the long-term results of this victimization can be severe. In several of the books listed in the bibliography, you will see that some of the most savage sex criminals were childhood victims of female perpetrators.

Female child molesters can "get by" with a lot of inappropriate sexual touching of very young children during bath time and helping them dress, etc., which would be dismissed as "care-taking" or "nurturing" activity if disclosed by the child. Yet if the same acts were committed by a man, they would be suspect. The key ingredient to determining if a sex crime has been committed *is that the perpetrator committed the acts for their own gratification, not for the benefit of the child nor with any regard for the impact it would have on the child.* In a clinical sense, these types of suspects can be fixated or regressed offenders, they can be rapists, they can operate within their own family or they can operate outside of the family, even assaulting strangers.

As the male child victim becomes older and the sexual contact becomes more involved, you have a sexual victimization of the male child by the adult female with the same dynamics as any other child molestation situation.

When an adult female is involved sexually with a teenage boy, the victim is often considered as "being lucky" to have a female adult teach him about sex. In reality, what is happening is that he is being sexually victimized the same as if he were being assaulted by a male suspect. If the roles were reversed and an adult male were having sex with a teenage female there would be no doubt in anybody's mind that it is wrong, and a crime is being committed. Society tends to condone this type of behavior and, as a result, the victim is compelled to suppress his feelings about the victimization, or if he does report, he is discounted and the severity of the impact of the incident diminished, often by those in positions of authority.

Generally speaking, men tend to express their negative feelings through anger. When a man feels anxiety, helplessness, loneliness, etc., he tends to try to express these feelings through angry behavior or by being "macho." In extreme cases, this anger is ultimately projected by the man, and in an attempt to displace all of these feelings and somehow relieve the tremendous feeling of low self-esteem, he strikes out in anger and then becomes, himself, a perpetrator, often a violent one.

Some experts believe that if a man has been emotionally, physically or sexually abused by a female, he will have a tendency to hate women in general because they are the cause of all of his bad feelings. He then tries to "get even" for all of these wrongs that have been done to him. It is through the projection of the anger that the adult male who was a child victim attempts to "get even." If he has learned to eroticize violence, you are now looking at the profile of a rapist. If that victim has not learned to eroticize violence, he may be someone who is continually getting into fights, even to the extreme of committing assaults with a deadly weapon—and even murders. In the mid-eighties a study was conducted at San Quentin which found that 100% of those incarcerated for violent crimes had been victims of child abuse. This is a significant fact to keep in mind before you discount any child's account of abuse of any nature.

I have spoken with several teenage boys who have been sexually assaulted by females. Many of them expressed tremendous fear and confusion about what was happening to them. They felt a complete lack of control over their bodies during the assaults and experienced great feelings of conflict and guilt about the incidents. If a male child is allowed to express those feelings and deal with them, as female victims are encouraged to do, then they will be able to cope with the victimization and move on with their life. However, as with all traumatic feeling suppression, there is a potential for disaster with regard to a person eventually acting out their anger and they could become a sexual predator. Lacking any sense of control in their own life, they attempt to use sexual assault as an opportunity to be in control.

EXAMPLE: ADULT FEMALE PERPETRATOR ADOLESCENT MALE VICTIM

Several years ago I investigated a case which profoundly displays the double standard thinking. A patrol officer found a parked car behind a closed industrial complex late one night. The seats were reclined in the vehicle and it appeared that he had stumbled across a couple of "lovers."

When the officer approached the vehicle, he found a fourteen-year-old boy, completely naked, sitting behind the wheel. Sitting next to him was a forty-year-old female teacher who was fully clothed. As soon as the officer approached the car, the female jumped out and spontaneously stated, "We didn't have time to do anything. We were going to do something sexual, but we didn't have time. You caught us too soon; we didn't do anything wrong." The officer was told that the boy's clothes were in the trunk, at which time he allowed the boy to retrieve his clothing and dress. While dressing, more information of what happened was revealed.

The schoolteacher stated that she was tutoring the boy and he snuck out of his house (at midnight) to meet her down the street from his residence. This was their normal routine. The female allowed the boy to drive her car (a privilege which is not uncommon for a pedophile to offer in exchange for the sexual activity) and they had gone somewhere to obtain something to eat. According to the female, the boy then spilled his meal onto his lap and had to remove all of his clothing and place it into the trunk of the car "because they would dry faster in the trunk than in the passenger compartment." (Sometimes it is hard for an officer to keep a straight face!) The officer learned that the boy's parents were aware of the relationship and had been trying to stop it for several months. However, they had been unsuccessful and the boy kept sneaking out at night and meeting with the teacher for this "special tutoring."

The officer told the schoolteacher that she would have to drive the car since the boy was unlicensed and that she should immediately take the boy home to his parents. He let them drive away and handled the whole incident on a field interview card.

When the situation was called to my attention, I contacted the school and learned that the teacher had been warned numerous times to stay away from not only this particular boy, but several others with whom she had been in contact over the last several years. The school administration had a requirement that she never close her classroom door and that she had been forbidden to work in a one-on-one situation with any of her male pupils because she had a tendency to "be too close" to her male students.

Holding the entire incident up to scrutiny, if the schoolteacher had been a male, and the fourteen-year-old been a female, a whole different outcome would have occurred. Obviously, the schoolteacher would have been arrested, the parents of the child would have been contacted to come pick up their daughter and criminal charges would have been filed—the double standard was certainly in effect.

I am sure there are some of you reading this, both male and female, who have some doubt as to whether or not the female schoolteacher "teaching" her pupil about sex was inappropriate and fail to see the potential traumatic effect it might have on the boy.

Think for a moment of how vulnerable you were at the age of twelve. Imagine being that age and being the constant unwilling sexual partner of your stepmother. Think of how you would feel every night, going to bed knowing that your stepmother would come in drunk at two or three in the morning and demand some type of sexual acts. *That scenario is a passage into terror, not a passage into manhood.* Compounding the impact is that while the male child may be dreading the moment the stepmother arrives, and experiencing remorse about the betrayal of his father, he finds himself lying in bed with a full erection. Aroused sex organs have no conscience—especially when a male is eleven or twelve. Conflicts with no possible solutions create mental imbalance. Hopefully, this helps you understand why such a male child victim could become such a violent adult.

CLANDESTINE TELEPHONE CALLS FROM VICTIMS

Victims of this age range are good candidates for making clandestine telephone calls to the suspects. They are old enough to understand the nature of the call, that being to solicit incriminating statements from the suspect. This type of call is only successful if the perpetrator is unaware that the child has come to the police department to report the offenses.

DATE RAPE

Females between the ages of thirteen and eighteen are prime candidates for date rape, or acquaintance rape scenarios. Because of the normal irresponsible behaviors of adolescents, they frequently get themselves into situations that they cannot get themselves out of. Often, they will either be hitchhiking or come in contact with a stranger when they are intoxicated or have been using drugs. Because of this, they find themselves being victimized quite routinely.

Suspects who commit such rapes are predators in the same sense as the person who commits a stranger-type abduction and rape. However, their choice of victims are those who are more vulnerable to attack because of their age and/or degree of intoxication.

Being the victim of this type of offense has an additional traumatizing effect to the victim since it attacks her ability to choose safe people to be around. So, in addition to the violation of the body and her ability to be in control of her body, she also now has to question her ability to choose safe friends.

SEX OF INTERVIEWER

My experience has been that it doesn't make any difference as to whether or not a male or female interviews any sexual assault victim. What is more important are the abilities of the individual interviewer/officer. I have seen some females who are very good interviewers; and I have seen some who are absolutely horrible. The same is true for male officers. To routinely think that a female victim would automatically feel more comfortable talking to a female officer is erroneous. There is also a school of thought that teaches a male officer might be the best to interview a female victim since it will help her to regain a feeling/sense that men are safe to be around after she has been victimized by a male. The concept of *Strength Through Association* will be discussed in more detail in subsequent chapters.

The most important quality of interviewing a victim is your ability to portray a professional image toward the victim. This professional need-to-know, no-nonsense image allows you to ask all of the sensitive, pertinent sexual questions that you need to know to fulfill your crime reporting requirements.

STRANGER RAPE

(Refer to Chapter 5 regarding Adult Victims)

MEDICAL EXAMS

Because many of these sexual offenses are accomplished with the threat of force or while the victim is unable to resist because of intoxication, often the only physical evidence will be found during the medical exam. (Refer to Chapter 5, Adult Victimization, for further details.)

FALSE REPORTS

In this age range, there are numerous reasons why someone might falsely report a rape. Many of these false reports are simply attempts to redirect attention away from something wrong that the victim has done so that he/she is not disciplined for coming home late, joy-riding in the family car, some sort of drug use, or violation of other household rules.

Sometimes the victim who has committed a violation of household rules will make up a story about being sexually assaulted in order to gain sympathy for the sexual assault, as opposed to being disciplined for violating household rules.

Other motivations for a false report would be someone who had a consensual sexual act but is afraid that they have now contracted a venereal disease or become pregnant and needed to explain the pregnancy or sexually transmitted disease to their family.

Fortunately, victims in this age range are not very sophisticated in coming up with a story about being victimized, and a detailed interview with them will reveal several discrepancies or holes in their story that will normally indicate if their report is false.

Chapter 5

INTERVIEWING AGES 18-80

Generally, victims in this age range are thought of as being one-time kidnap and rape victims, or victims of random sexual assault as opposed to an ongoing type of victimization that you see with children. (The only exception to this would be in spousal abuse/rape cases which will be discussed later.)

WHEN THE SUSPECT IS A STRANGER

First contact

In this type of case, generally the first contact with the victim is via the 911 emergency line where she or a friend has called in to report the sexual assault. The 911 tape is a critical evidence item. The spontaneous statements exception to the hearsay rule in the California Evidence Code allows such 911 tapes, along with spontaneous statements made to witnesses immediately after the assault, to be used as evidence.(See your individual state codes.) You should request from your communications supervisor that a copy of the 911 tape be maintained for evidence.

Also, be sure to contact any "fresh complaint" witnesses. This could include a husband, boyfriend, parent, or anyone that the victim contacted prior to actually calling the police department. Also, emergency room nurses and doctors can fall within this exception to the hearsay rule as "fresh complaint witnesses." If the victim makes a spontaneous statement to them, this can be used in court to help corroborate her statement.

Stalking

Generally speaking, sexual predators do not follow one particular victim for an extended length of time prior to committing a sexual assault. Although I am sure it does happen on rare occasions, generally speaking, the sexual predator does not have the impulse control to delay immediate gratification of his needs for several months or years. It would be extremely rare for one victim to be stalked by a total stranger for an extended length of time for the purpose of sexual assault or for repeated sexual assaults by the same suspect. The classical stalker is generally obsessed with an individual for other than sexual reasons. Usually their obsession stems from broken romances to problems in the workplace or even celebrities.

Predator Rapist

In general terms, the rapist/sexual predator is seeking to level a balance beam scale in his head. When the scale is balanced, he acts normally and does not assault. As he starts to get out of tilt because of some real or perceived wrongs in his life, he begins to fantasize about raping someone, which gives him a feeling of power, which helps balance the scale. As he becomes increasingly out of kilter, he begins to act out on his fantasies.

The associated fantasy is that the suspect will assault a woman and this sexual experience will be overwhelmingly positive for both the suspect and the victim and that both the suspect and the victim will fall madly in love with each other and they will ride off into the sunset together and live happily ever after. Unfortunately for the suspect, this never happens. The victim never falls madly in love with him and frequently the suspect has difficulty maintaining an erection or actually achieving ejaculation.

The rape does satisfy the need for power, control and domination over the victim, but does not satisfy a basic sexual need, as most of society would see it. As a result, the suspect sees the victim as having failed, since she was not sexy enough, involved enough in the sexual assault, or there was something wrong with the victim that caused the fantasy to be unfulfilled.

Because of this combination of fantasy versus balancing the power/emotion scale in the suspect's head, it would be very unlikely for a suspect to follow and continually sexually assault the same victim over and over again because *she* has failed to fulfill his fantasy.

Also, the unbalancing of the emotional scale inside the suspect's head happens very quickly. For that reason, he needs an immediate solution to his dilemma, that being his inability to deal with his own emotions. As a result, he will basically grab a victim of convenience or opportunity.

What is more likely to take place is that a rapist, when the scales are slightly out of whack, will start to prowl the neighborhood in which he lives. This kind of suspect finds large apartment complexes the same as shopping malls for him, since he will continually prowl the complex to look for victims. He will know every open window; he will know every female who lives in those apartment; he will know when they are alone and when their husbands are at home; he will know every crack in the Venetian blinds that he can peek through to get a glimpse of a potential victim.

Generally, this peeking and prowling process helps stabilize the emotional teeter totter in his head since the fantasy about being able to break in and rape the victim will, most times, satisfy the emotional need for power and control over the victim. It is only when the scale is tipped drastically that he actually acts out on the fantasy and breaks into the apartment and rapes.

It is more likely that your average rapist has a general idea of many potential victims in the immediate area where he lives. If he finds the need on a particular night to act out on the sexual fantasy, he will know which victim he can go to on that particular date and time, since he will know who is available, and he can go in and assault them at that time.

This same type of suspect, when he finds the need to fantasize about controlling a woman, might prowl the freeways or the supermarket parking lots for potential victims. This is the type of person who will see a potential victim driving alone on the freeway and will start following her for an extended length of time. He will follow her and fantasize about being able to rape her. If he actually follows her to her home, he might wait outside for a while, again fantasizing about the rape and, in essence, working up the nerve to carry out the sexual assault. He may then approach the victim with some sort of a ruse, such as knocking on the door and claiming to be the TV repairman, or the man from the Gas Company, etc. to make entry and then capture the victim and follow through with the sexual assault.

He may also find a victim he is attracted to at the supermarket and may follow her home and assault her in a similar fashion.

Because of this, it is important to obtain background information from the victim as to what their activities were prior to the sexual assault, going back at least several hours prior to the actual capture by the suspect. You might want to go back 24 hours through the victim's routine and find out if sometime during that 24 hours, there might have been a time when she came into contact with the suspect.

If the attack occurs in a neighborhood or apartment complex where the victim has lived for some time, you should ask her if she is aware of any complaints from other neighbors about people peeking in their windows or theft of lingerie from the laundry rooms. You should also make contact with the apartment manager to see if they are aware of similar complaints. The manager may also be aware of prowlers or other nuisance crimes that the victim is not aware of.

Since rape involves the control of the victim by the suspect, it would not be unusual for a suspect to break into an unoccupied residence where a female lives by herself and, in essence, control her property by stealing her underwear or being inside her bedroom where he can fantasize about being able to rape her if she had actually been home. He might go so far as to masturbate over her bed or onto her clothing. The apartment managers may be aware of these types of crimes occurring within the complex prior to the actual rape of the victim that you are interviewing.

There are several different types of rapists, as defined by Dr. Nicholas Groth and others. (Refer to the bibliography and Part II of this book for more details and further readings on this subject.)

Modus Operandi vs. Fantasy of Rapist

Modus operandi (or MO) generally refers to the method in which a suspect robs a bank or breaks into a house to commit a burglary. Generally, in those types of crimes, you don't have to go beyond the MO to help you identify the motivating factor in the crime, that being obtaining money. However, in sex offenses, the MO is considerably different from that of a property crime.

In sex offenses, MO is that tactic, or technique, that brings the suspect into contact with the victim. These approaches can be simple or ingenious. They range from calling an escort service to his house, use of a dating service to make contact with women, the use of "date rape drugs", or pretending to be a doctor needing to "inject" a special medicine into the victim via his penis. It can be as simple as breaking into her house, holding a gun to her head and raping her, or kidnapping her off the street at knife-point. Whatever the approach, it's only the first step in achieving the true motive of the crime.

Once the suspect has been successful in capturing the female, then the secondary phase of the assault takes place, and this is the actual fantasy phase in which the suspect acts out the fantasy as to how he wants the assault to take place. The fantasies can be very basic or they can be quite elaborate.

Six Phases of a Sexual Assault

Everything the suspect does during the actual sexual assault means something to him. It may not mean anything to you, the interviewer, but it is of great importance to the suspect. With that in mind, if the victim tells you something that seems rather bizarre, be sure it gets documented. It may become very important later. If possible, during your investigation you should identify the following phases of the sexual assault. These are:

1. The Approach Phase: This may involve following the victim home from the supermarket, prowling her apartment complex or meeting her in a bar.

2. Contact: The suspect may confront her at knife point in the carports, break into the residence and confront her in bed, or pull a weapon on a hitchhiker or prostitute.

3. Capture: The capture of the victim is actually complete once she decides to submit to the sexual assault, as opposed to being killed or seriously injured. Perhaps 70% to 90% of suspects will use only enough force to capture the victim.

There are suspects who actually enjoy inflicting physical pain to the victim and these are the ones who use an excessive amount of force to capture the victim and will continue to beat or stab the victim far beyond what is necessary to capture her for the purpose of the sexual assault.

An exception to this capture-submission phase is when the victim is rendered unconscious by drugs or physical force.

4. Assault Phase: This is the actual assault itself and may include a great deal of dialogue by the suspect directing the victim to do or say certain things during the rape.

5. Post-Assault Behavior: During this phase, the suspect will sometimes be apologetic to the victim, often trying to explain to her why he needed to rape her, there by justifying his actions. The excuses are normally lies, but they usually consist of statements such as, "My girlfriend just broke up with me," or "My girlfriend is pregnant and I haven't had sex in a long time." It is not unusual in a post assault phase for the suspect to get the victim something to drink, ask her for her telephone number, carry on some general conversation, cuddle with her, or perhaps tell her how to better secure her house in the future so no one else will break in.

6. Escape Phase: This is when the suspect actually terminates contact with the victim and flees. In a burglary-rape situation, it is not unusual for him to have prepared an exit prior to his actually using it, e.g., he will break in through a window, but prior to making contact with the victim, he will unlock the front door for a quick escape.

He may have a vehicle parked nearby to aid in his escape, or if he lives nearby he will simply flee on foot. Identifying his escape route is important for locating evidence he may have discarded along the way.

The six phases of the assault should normally be obtained during the victim interview. They are important in the suspect interview in that they tell you a lot about the suspect, including what type of offender he is. This is fundamental information before starting the suspect interview.

Age of Victim

Most suspects are very opportunistic in their selection of victims. Basically, when they feel the need to rape, they will grab a victim of opportunity providing a wide age range in which they will sexually assault. Since the suspect sees the victim as an entity to possess, as opposed to a real person, he really doesn't care about the age of the victim. I have seen the same suspect attack victims between the ages of 11 and 80, all of the women being victims of opportunity.

However, due to the emotional make-up of these suspects, a lot of them do not feel very adequate when dealing with women. Sometimes, you will see a suspect in this category who will only assault very young children and/or the elderly. Both of these groups, young children and the elderly, are seen as non-sexual beings. Since society generally does not think of children as having any sort of sexual knowledge or experiences, the suspect does not have to perform adequately for this child and, as a result, he can assault them without a fear of being laughed at because of his inability to satisfy the victim. Also in our society, grandmothers are not considered to be sexual beings and for that reason, the same suspect who is raping children, may see an elderly victim as being a non-sexual person for whom he does not have to perform adequately. For this reason, he may assault this population group also.

Perpetrator's Rape Kits

Sometimes, suspects will prepare a rape kit to take with them on their sexual assault adventures. This will involve a backpack or duffel bag that will contain tools they may need to use in order to accomplish the rape.

You may find a ski mask, gloves, duct tape, handcuffs, guns, knives, pry tools, etc. in this rape kit that may be carried around by the suspect to help him in capturing a victim. To some suspects, the actual acquiring of these items is a part of the fantasy and, in essence, a part of the "date" prior to the sexual assault. Some of them carry the rape kit around with them to help them fantasize about raping a woman of opportunity. It helps them with the fantasy process to know that they have the tools available to them to commit a sexual assault if they choose to do so.

Rapists are masters at fantasizing. They have taken the ability to fantasize in order to stabilize the balance beam in their head to an absolute extreme. Anything that aids them in this fantasy, such as the rape kit, will help them in balancing the emotional scale in their head.

Keep in mind that just because a person is a rapist (or a child molester), it does not exclude him from being another kind of criminal also. The rapist can be a bank robber, a burglar, can write bad checks, be a drug user, or all of the above. When investigating these types of crimes, if you were to come across a "rape kit", or any other items that might make you believe the person you are dealing with is a rapist, be sure to take those items of evidence, or at least document them and see to it that the sex crimes investigators are aware of who this person is so that they might link him to unsolved crimes.

Rape Trauma Syndrome

The emotional and physical symptoms experienced by rape victims have been analyzed and assembled into a group called the Rape Trauma Syndrome. (Refer to Appendix "A")

The initial response to being sexually assaulted is a denial of the emotional impact of the assault on the victim. Because of this, a lot of victims will show a very flat or negative affect when you initially approach them. The victim may be upset and crying when you first arrive, but once she realizes that she is safe with you, don't be alarmed if she shuts off all expressions of emotion and becomes very easy to interview.

Since the victim will probably want to deny the emotional impact of the assault, it makes for an easy interview because they will become very matter-of-fact during the interview process itself. However, when you get to the actual sexual assault, i.e., the actual vaginal penetration, or the actual initiation of oral sex, often the memory of that act overpowers them and, once again, they will break down and start to cry or visibly shake. Be sure to document these emotions during your police report because *you* have now become a spontaneous statement witness and, per the exception to the Evidence Code, you can now testify as to the victim's emotional state at the time you contacted them.

INTERVIEW: RAPE VICTIM

Normally, in a one-time rape situation when you are called immediately to the location, you, as a police officer, will contain the initial crime scene, have additional officers set up a perimeter, and then conduct a crime scene search for evidence and obtain a suspect description. This process is exactly the same as it would be for any sort of in-progress or recently committed crime that you might respond to.

In the sexual assault, however, you normally want to get the victim to a hospital where you can be sure her medical needs are being taken care of. Often, the interview with the victim takes place at the hospital while you are waiting for the doctor to be available to examine her.

In this type of situation, the victim is very much aware of why you are there and is aware that you are going to interview her about what took place. Explain to the victim that you are going to spend a lot of time talking to her, but that you are going to spend *most* of the time talking about what led up to the actual sexual assault, this being the approach, contact, and capture phase, as opposed to spending a great deal of time on the actual sexual assault itself. Tell her that you are very interested in what the suspect said during the time they were in contact with each other and in what his post-assault behaviors were. This allows the victim to relax a little bit, since she won't have to spend hours talking about the actual physical penetration of her body, which is normally what the public fears the police interview in a rape situation involves.

You have to convey to the victim that you have a *legitimate need* to know the information that you are going to be asking and to assure her that you are not going to go back to the station and talk about her victimization as if you had just seen an X-rated movie. Once the victim feels comfortable in talking to you, the interview is generally quite easy.

After relaying basic suspect information to assisting officers, you need to settle into the long-term interviewing process with the victim. You can start off by asking the victim what she has done in the last several hours, i.e., if she has returned home from a date, if she was at the supermarket, if she returned directly home from work, or if she had just gotten up in the morning, etc. This eases you into the interview process and gives you the information you might need as to where she has been and where she might have first been observed by the suspect.

Keep in mind that the victim may not be aware of the first time that the suspect actually observed her. For that reason, you want to advise her of this and simply tell her that it is possible that the suspect followed her home, or possibly someone in the neighborhood that she hasn't thought of as a potential suspect. During this interview process, she may suddenly realize that there was someone who contacted her several hours earlier at the market or was following her home on the freeway and she has not made the connection between that initial contact and the sexual assault.

When questioning her about the first contact between her and the suspect, you need to find out what physically happened, such as he broke in through a window, or he knocked on the front door and pretended to be a repairman, or he approached her on the sidewalk with a gun in his hand. But you also need to ask her what his demeanor was like. Ask her if he was in a heightened state of anxiety, if he was breathing heavily, if he was apologetic or very angry, and at what point in time this demeanor changed, if it did, during the contact he had with her. Frequently, a suspect will be in a state of very high anxiety at the time he makes initial contact with the victim, but once he has been successful in capturing her, he may become more relaxed. What the victim might mistake as being a relaxed state is more likely the suspect entering the fantasy phase of the rape scenario.

You also need to ask the victim if the suspect only used enough force to successfully capture her. One of the elements of a forcible rape is that the suspect overcame any resistance by the victim by using force, fear, or the threat of great bodily injury. You need to obtain details from the victim that fulfills this element of the crime. Basically, if the victim tells you that she was afraid she was going to be killed because the suspect put a gun in her face and said he would kill her if she did not comply, then obviously that fulfills that element. Often, the simple size difference between the suspect and victim is enough for her to feel this fear element and a need to comply out of fear of being severely beaten by the suspect.

It is important to explain to the victim that every time a sexual act took place, that a separate and distinct crime has occurred. If the suspect initially inserts a finger into the victim's vagina, that is a separate felony. If he then performed oral sex on her, that is also a separate felony. If she performed oral sex on him, that is another separate felony. If he has intercourse with her, that is also a separate felony. Each time a different felony is committed, these crimes can be charged separately against the suspect and he is sentenced separately on each act. Most sexual assaults involve several felonies perpetrated on the victim. In an average rape case, the suspect may have committed several individual sexual assaults on the victim in addition to, perhaps, kidnapping or falsely imprisoning her, or using a firearm during the course of the assault which may result in an enhanced sentence. You need to explain to the victim that the reason you want the details about the sexual assault is so you can document each of these individual crimes so that the suspect's prison sentence will increase with each crime.

Once the victim understands this, she should have no problem in telling you what took place. Occasionally, she will be upset with having had to perform a sexual act that she finds is particularly distasteful, and you need to be sensitive to her feelings. But generally speaking, they will be very forthright with what took place.

If a victim is having difficulty remembering the sequence of events as they unfolded during the assault phase, you may want to interview her starting from the last contact with the perpetrator, working backward in time. You explain this to her by saying that it might be very easy for her to recite the alphabet from A to Z, but if she were to try to recite the alphabet backwards, from Z to A, she would have to stop and think about each letter as she was going backwards to be sure that she got it in the proper sequence. The same thing is true for recalling the actual sexual assault itself if she is a little confused about which event happened first. If you can take her backwards through the event, sometimes it forces her to think about them in a little more detail and you can get a little clearer picture as to what took place.

There is no real reason to "overkill" the actual sexual acts themselves. If the victim tells you that the suspect had an erection and placed his erect penis into her vagina, that satisfies the elements of the crime. If you can get an approximate length of time the intercourse took place, such as two minutes, three minutes, five minutes, etc., that's fine, but it isn't overly important as far as the actual elements of a crime are concerned. The same thing holds true for rape with a foreign object. If the suspect puts one finger inside of the victim's vagina, two fingers, or three fingers, it really doesn't change the elements of the crime any. If the victim can recall if it was one or two fingers, that's fine, but don't belabor these types of points with them. I have seen many interviewers get so tied up in trying to figure out whether the suspect put one or two fingers inside of the victim, that it became burdensome to the point of being absurd.

I have also seen interviewers go on at great length to try to ascertain if the victim knew if the suspect ejaculated. Whether or not a suspect ejaculated during the vaginal intercourse with the victim is not an element of the crime. It has absolutely no importance as far as the law is concerned. It does have some importance as to finding biological evidence that might help identify the suspect, but that is really its only importance.

Since the suspect ejaculating is only important as far as collecting physical evidence is concerned, you should explain this to the victim and then ask her where the biological evidence might be, such as on her clothing or inside her body, on the bedding, on the car seat or on the floor.

If the suspect is having difficulty maintaining an erection during the sexual assault, you need to document this in as much detail as possible. You need to correspond his lack of being able to maintain an erection with what did he do to resolve that problem, such as masturbate himself, or have the victim perform oral sex on him, and what his demeanor or mood was like at these times. Did he become apologetic? Did he become angry?

The victims ability to explain the suspect's actions, demeanor, and words used as the assault is continuing, is very helpful in discovering what his fantasy is. Most suspects will act out the same fantasy several times and then after four or five sexual assaults, the fantasy will change somewhat.

Since we know that MO and fantasy are two separate things, it is quite possible that a particular suspect will come into contact with victims in a different fashion. If a rape suspect has an MO that is working for him, he will try to stay with it. But the opportunistic nature of this type of individual may result in a momentary change in MO/contact. Just because a suspect breaks into a house and confronts a victim in her bed at 3:00 a.m., puts a knife to her throat and rapes her, doesn't mean that he won't also rape a hitchhiker, or that he won't rape a prostitute, or a woman working for an out-call service who comes to his house. He may have several different MOs that bring him in contact with potential victims. However, the fantasy that he acts out once he has captured the victim will quite often be the same or very similar.

It is very helpful in identifying suspects who have committed multiple offenses through the fantasy if the patrol officer can try to detail the mood and terminology used during the sexual assault. For example, he might call the victim a "bitch" or a "whore" while she is performing oral sex on him, but when he is performing vaginal intercourse with her, he may want her to repeat phrases like, "You're the best lover I've every had," or, "You have the biggest penis I've ever had." This is very important terminology for identifying offenders later on.

It is not unusual for a suspect, after he has captured a victim, to appear as if he is reading from a script as the sexual assault goes on. Frequently, the suspect has fantasized the rape scenario over and over so many times in his mind that he wants it to occur specifically as he has rehearsed it. If you can elicit from the victim as to whether or not the suspect went into a phase where it appeared he was reading from an invisible script, this may be very helpful in identifying who he is later on.

Male vs. Female Interviewers

It has been my experience that the sex of the interviewer has absolutely no bearing on the quality of information obtained from the victim. What is more important is the interviewer's ability to establish a rapport and the serious approach required to obtain the information from the victim. There is also a school of thought that says that a male interviewer talking to a female rape victim is very therapeutic for the female. This allows the female to have a safe contact with a male who is in a position of power, who is not going to victimize her, which begins the process of rebuilding her ability to trust men. This *Strength Through Association* helps start the recovery process and helps build rapport between the officer and the victim.

Obviously, if you have a rape victim who wishes to be interviewed by a female officer, by all means do what you can to oblige her request. However, it has been my experience that this really is not a problem and most victims feel perfectly comfortable talking to a male about the sexual assault, as long as it is done properly.

False Rape Reports

False reporting of rapes is a bigger problem than most people realize. It has become such a problem that the FBI has developed a profile of the person who falsely reports a sexual assault. A copy of that profile is attached in Appendix "B" and should be reviewed by the reader at this time.

I have encountered many fictitious rapes that can be listed in several broad categories, as listed below. This does not mean that any rape that has some of these characteristics is a false report. Some of the motivating factors I have come across are:

A. Intoxication: This is when a female becomes so intoxicated by drugs and/or alcohol that she wakes up with the "wrong guy."

B. Pregnant/STD: This is when a female fears she has become pregnant or has contracted a sexually transmitted disease during consensual sex, but is afraid to tell her parents, boyfriend or husband how "it" actually happened.

C. Attention: This type is seeking attention, not only from the police department, but from friends and relatives. People who fall into this category often have elaborate stories about having been stalked by the suspect for an extended length of time. They are also notorious for "late" reporting their sexual victimization. This is also the type of person who would be more likely to self-inflict injuries to corroborate her allegation of rape.

D. Misdirection: This type diverts attention away from some violation of household rules (normally a teenager violating curfew). She will state that the reason she came home late was because she was raped, gaining sympathy from her parents instead of being punished.

E. Homeward Bound: This victim has moved out of her family's home to be "on her own," but finds that it is too difficult. However she doesn't want to admit this, so she fabricates a rape, normally occurring in her new apartment, in order to get the family to "force" her to return home.

F. Broken Lease: In order to break a rental agreement, the victim will report that someone has broken into her home and sexually assaulted her. She then tells that landlord that she is too fearful to live there any longer and needs to be allowed to get out of the lease agreement. A variation of this is when the rent money has been spent on drugs and the victim reports that someone broke into the apartment stole the rent money and raped her. This allows her to not pay the upcoming month's rent and then break the lease.

G. Sympathy/Guilt: These victims have recently broken up with a boyfriend or husband and will report that they were assaulted to gain a sympathy or guilt reaction. When successful, the ex-mate will come running back to protect her from the rapist.

H. Cheating Wife: This woman is having an affair and has in essence "overslept" and does not return home on time. She will fictitiously report a rape to account for her time away from home. This also "covers" any pregnancy or STD she may have acquired.

I. Copycat: This type is similar to the attention seeker and surfaces during a series of legitimate rapes that have received a lot of news media attention. This woman will report that she too has been attacked by the same cat burglar or stalker. This is another reason why it is important to carefully document the statements made by the suspect during the capture and assault phases of the legitimate rapes. You then have to keep this information away from the news media so it is not commonly known. This way, when the copycat victim surfaces, she will not be able to tell a story that is consistent with the other, legitimate, victims.

J. Mentally Ill: This category has several sub-categories.

1. Extremely Mentally Disturbed Case: This person has extreme form(s) of mental illness which causes her to fictitiously report a rape or other crime.

2. Emotion Turmoil: This person needs to reach out for some sort of psychological help but doesn't know how to do so in a more legitimate fashion. They need to escape from the source of stress in their lives so they make up a rape story that allows them to do so, without "losing face" to their family and friends. An example of this would be a college student who is under a tremendous amount of pressure from herself and family to be a very high achiever. If the pressure from this high performance becomes overwhelming, she will fabricate a rape or stalker in order to allow her to flee the academic environment in order to get away from the attacker. This is very similar to the HOMEWARD BOUND type.

When dealing with these people, you have to be careful not to "push them over the edge." Because of their mental instability, being confrontational (calling them a liar) might cause them to commit suicide. You might suggest that they seek counseling for the "rape." A good counselor will be able to target the real problem, reduce the stress and the stalker will disappear.

3. Historical/Survivor: Occasionally an adult who has been the victim of childhood incest will falsely report a rape. This is because they need to talk about a sexual issue in their life, but can't yet disclose the incest. Decades of burying the truth and fearing that no one will believe them forces them to make up a story about a current sexual victimization. This opens the door for them to talk about their emotional problems surrounding sexual issues.

Again, when dealing with someone like this, you have to be careful not to "push them over the edge" and into suicide. Since you, *AS AN OFFICER*, are in a position of power, as was their father who molested them, you should not confront them with the "lie." It's much better to direct them to counseling so the real issues can be addressed.

This means that you'll have to take the rape report, which will waste a few hours of your time. However, an officer (usually male) doing and saying the right thing to someone like this is the ethical thing to do and is another example of *STRENGTH THROUGH ASSOCIATION.*

4. The Exhibitionist: A true female exhibitionist can drive a police department crazy. They will hang out at the cop-stop and "show it all" to everyone on the graveyard shift, which sometimes ends with disciplinary action being taken against the officers. The same woman will parade half naked in their living rooms with the drapes open for all to see. They will also make false rape reports. These reports will be in the form of "woman down" calls. The officer will arrive to find the nude victim lying unconscious on the floor, with no head trauma. She miraculously regains consciousness after all of swing swift and half the fire department has seen her naked, and reports that she was struck on the head, from behind, by an unknown assailant, who must have removed her clothing and raped her. If you come across one of these types of "victims," don't interview her alone!

Fortunately, most of the fictitious rape reports don't have an identifiable suspect attached to the allegation. Most of the time the victim will create a situation in which she will not or cannot identify the suspect and there will be no leads, witnesses or physical evidence that might lead to a suspect.

An example of this is the woman who reports that she was approached in broad daylight, at the busiest intersection in town and dragged off by a suspect, whom she did not get a good look at, and was raped. She cannot give a description of the assailant nor can any witnesses be found.

Another example would be the suspect who wore a ski mask (in the middle of summer) and gloves and while holding the victim down with both his hands, managed to put on a condom before he raped her. Have you ever tried to put on a condom while wearing gloves?

The use of condoms by rapists is now quite common. They are aware of DNA evidence (it's probably what sent them to prison the first time) and they are fearful of getting a STD during the rape. The suspect using a condom does not mean that the report is false.

It is also common to see a delay in reporting of the rape in these fictitious cases. This allows the victim time to have laundered any evidence items or clothing and for her memory of the suspect to fade. In the case of the victim being pregnant or catching a STD, it takes a few weeks for these symptoms to develop, resulting in the late report.

A very general rule of thumb is that if the rape report sounds like a TV movie, then it's probably fictitious. Since the general public has no idea as to how real rapists actually think and act, they tend to make up a story based on what they have seen on television.

I want to restate, as strongly as possible, that just because a victim reports a rape that has one or more of these elements in it, it does not automatically mean that the report is false. However, the investigating officer needs to be aware of this possibility and, when appropriate, explore this possibility. This is done by asking general inquiry questions or background question of the victim, such as:

"How long have you lived here?"

"Do you have a boyfriend or husband?"

"Have you broken up with a boyfriend or husband?"

"Has anything like this happened to you before?"

These are phrased as general inquiry or background, as opposed to accusatory questions . They will frequently solicit the type of information that is helpful in establishing if a report is false or not.

CHAPTER 5   INTERVIEWING AGES 18-80

In a legitimate rape report, the victim will be able to give you associated details about the assault. These are the same kind of details that the child will be able to give about a molestation allegation.

Rape Reports: Making it "Better Than it is"

Sometimes, officers feel the need to make the victim's activity at the time of a crime sound better than it actually was. What occurred *is not your responsibility; your responsibility is simply to document what took place.* If a victim tells you that she was drunk or had been using drugs, or had multiple sex partners prior to the rape, you simply have to document that. Don't feel that you have an obligation to "clean up" the victim. If she was dancing seductively on the night club dance floor with the suspect a few minutes prior to him raping her in the parking lot, then say that. There is no need to cover it up or downplay it.

Sample Report Narrative: Stranger Rape

On August 3, 1997, at 0230 hours, I met with victim #97-123 (referred to as "victim") at her apartment. She told me that she had been sexually assaulted by someone who had broken into her apartment. I initially obtained a suspect description and his last known direction of travel and broadcast that information to assisting officers, who set up a perimeter and conducted an area search for the suspect.

I noticed that the victim had a bruised right eye, as if she had been punched in the face, and that her nose was bleeding slightly. There was also some swelling to the right side of her face. She was initially treated at the scene by paramedics and then transported to Martin Luther Hospital in Anaheim for medical follow-up and for an ASAV exam. I made arrangements for Officer Brown and for CSI officers to stay at the apartment where the crime had taken place to collect physical evidence and to photograph the scene.

Once I re-contacted the victim at the hospital, I took her into the doctors' lounge so I could interview her prior to the actual medical exam taking place.

The victim told me that yesterday, as is her normal routine, she got up at 6:30 a.m., prepared herself for work, and then went to work where she has a clerical position at a large factory. She stayed at work until about 5:00 p.m., at which time she returned to her residence to change clothes.

At about 6:30 p.m., she left her home to meet with a friend, Mary Smith, at the shopping mall. At the mall, the victim and her friend had dinner and then they shopped for several hours. The victim indicated she left the mall at around 9:30 p.m. and drove home. On the way home, she stopped at the Mobil gas station, one-half mile from her residence, to obtain gas prior to actually returning to her apartment. When she drove into the complex itself, she entered through the security gate and then parked in her assigned carport. The victim does not recall anyone following her home at this time. She then locked her car and walked directly to her apartment. Once she entered the apartment, shortly after 10:00 p.m., she locked the dead bolt lock behind her.

She said that she then prepared herself for bed. She actually went to bed around 11:00 p.m. wearing a long nightshirt and panties. She told me that she left the ground floor sliding glass patio door open about six inches for ventilation when she went to bed.

The victim also told me that she was watching television, as she normally did when she went to bed, and she normally falls asleep with the television on.

She said that she was awakened at around 2:30 a.m. when she felt a hand across her face. This startled her and she tried to sit up in bed. When she did this, she was struck in the face several times by the suspect.

The victim said that the suspect then told her to be quiet, while he held a knife in his right hand in front of her face. At this point, she noted that the suspect had taken a bath towel from out of the bathroom and actually covered up the television screen with it. The television itself was still on, but the light coming from the TV screen was now not sufficient enough for her to get a good look at his face. The victim told me that she was fearful that the suspect might kill her if she did not comply with his demands.

He then took her by the arm and had her get out of bed. While holding the knife to her throat, he walked her through the apartment to ensure that no one else was there. During this time, he asked her if she lived alone and if she had a boyfriend. She replied that she does have a boyfriend, but that he does not live at that location, and there was no one else living in the apartment. While being taken through the apartment by the suspect, she saw that the sliding glass door was now standing wide open.

While the suspect was walking her through the apartment, he seemed very nervous and agitated. He talked to her in a very demeaning fashion and demanded to know the last time she had "fucked" her boyfriend.

The suspect then walked the victim back into the bedroom, at which time he ordered her to take her clothing off. Once she was nude, he told her to lie on her back on the bed. He continued to demand that she not look at him and that she keep her eyes closed.

The suspect then loosened his belt, unbuttoned his jeans, and dropped his pants down to his ankles. He was also wearing a button-up-the-front dress shirt that he did not remove or unbutton. The victim said that she saw that the suspect did not have an erection. He put the knife down on the night stand and then began to masturbate himself. The suspect still had difficulty in gaining an erection and, at this point, he became very agitated and called the victim a "bitch" and "whore." He then demanded that she begin to masturbate herself in front of him. Initially, the victim refused, but as the suspect approached her and said he would kill her if she did not comply, she began to fondle her vaginal area as directed by the suspect.

After doing this for perhaps a minute or two, the suspect was able to gain an erection. The suspect then attempted to have vaginal intercourse with the victim by lying on top of her; however, he was unable to maintain an erection and actual intercourse was not achieved at this time.

The suspect again became angry and agitated and demanded that the victim perform oral sex on him. She sat up on the edge of the bed and, with the suspect standing in front of her, he ordered that she put his penis into her mouth. She stated that she complied and performed oral sex on the suspect for perhaps a minute to a minute and a half.

During this time, the suspect began to stroke the victim's hair and stated, "I know you love it, baby, I know you love it." The victim indicated that the suspect then told her to lie back down on the bed. At this time, she saw that his demeanor had changed and that he was now less agitated than before and was acting somewhat robot-like in his actions and his demeanor with her. The suspect told the victim to lie back down on the bed, at which time he began to perform oral sex on her. The victim said that the suspect placed his mouth on her vagina for perhaps two to three minutes.

The suspect then lay on top of the victim and was successful in penetrating her vagina with his penis. She stated that they had intercourse for a short length of time, and then he got off from on top of her and stopped having intercourse with her. He then told her to roll over onto her stomach, at which time he then penetrated her vagina from the rear. The victim stated they had intercourse in this position for perhaps two to three more minutes. During this time, the suspect told her to repeat the phrase, "You're the best; you're the best I've ever had."

The suspect then withdrew his penis from her body and had the victim sit on the edge of the bed as he masturbated himself in front of her. He then ejaculated onto the carpeting adjacent to the bed itself.

The suspect then pulled his pants back up but did not allow the victim to dress herself. He then asked her where her jewelry box was, at which point she directed him toward the dresser on the opposite side of the bedroom. He then went to the dresser and took a 14 karat gold necklace with a small heart-shaped pendant on it from out of the jewelry box and placed it in his pocket.

The suspect then had the victim, who was still nude, walk from the bedroom area into the living room, where he had her sit on the sofa. The suspect then explained to the victim that his girlfriend was pregnant and had not had sex in several months. He was somewhat apologetic in his statements to her, but told her that he was always very careful to be sure not to hurt anyone when he had sex with them. He also demanded that the victim repeat the phrase, "It's okay. I wanted to have sex with you. You didn't hurt me." After repeating this phrase to the suspect several times, the suspect stated that he was going to leave. He also told her that she should not leave her sliding glass door open in the future. The suspect then left via the front door.

The victim stated that when the suspect left by the front door, he did not unlock the dead bolt lock in order to exit, indicating that he must have unlocked this door prior to making first contact with the victim.

The victim said that she did not hear or see a vehicle leaving the area after the suspect fled her apartment. The victim added that once the suspect was outside of the apartment, she went to the front door and closed and locked it to ensure that he would not return. The victim stated she then called her boyfriend, Jeff Jones, and told him that she had been raped. The boyfriend, who lives several miles away, told the victim to hang up the phone and call "911" in order to get the police to respond immediately to her home.

Dr. Smith performed the medical examination on the victim. He later told me that there was evidence of vaginal trauma that was consistent with the history given by the victim. The medical staff also treated the victim for her blackened eye and bloody nose, but stated that these injuries were superficial and not life-threatening. The doctor supplied me with the rape kit evidence that he had obtained during the examination of the victim, which I booked into evidence at the police department.

The hospital staff had called the county's Victim-Witness Office, who had a worker respond to the hospital. Also, the victim's sister was contacted and came to the hospital with some fresh clothing. The clothing that the victim wore to the hospital was taken for evidentiary purposes. After the medical exam was completed, the victim left the hospital with her sister and the Victim-Witness counselor.

I also relayed the information back to the officers at the victim's apartment as to the location of the possible evidence (seminal fluid) on the floor next to the bed and the information that a necklace had been taken from the jewelry box and that the suspect had prepared an exit prior to committing the actual rape.

The victim also indicated that the last time she had consensual intercourse was perhaps eight to ten days ago with her boyfriend.

DATE RAPE / ACQUAINTANCE RAPE

Date rape suspects are sexual predators just as stranger rapists are, however, they have a slightly different method of operation. You can liken the difference between a date rape versus the stranger rape to a con man who commits a theft by fraud versus a bank robber who takes over a bank at gunpoint and steals money from the tellers. In the date rape scenario, the suspect is more like the con man who makes contact with the victim and then waits until the victim is particularly vulnerable, such as intoxicated, before he attempts a sexual assault.

Because of this acquaintance/prior relationship between the victim and suspect, these cases are more difficult to prosecute. It is quite possible that the victim has had prior consensual sex with the suspect or she has been in a relationship with the suspect that would tend to make people believe that the relationship has been sexual in nature. Quite often, the date rape scenario involves a situation where the victim has been drinking and/or using drugs and may have been doing this with the suspect.

Frequently, the sexual assault itself has the same dynamics as the stranger rape. The difference comes in the way the suspect approaches, contacts, and captures the victim. Once the capture is complete, the suspect may act out the same sort of rape fantasy that the stranger suspect has.

Because of the similarities, you interview the date rape victim in the same fashion as you would the victim of a stranger rape. You start with the first contact between her and the suspect and continue through the actual assault itself and the post-assault behavior.

Many of these date rape scenarios are not reported immediately. However, if the incident is reported within 72 hours of the actual sexual assault, you need to take the victim to the hospital for a sexual assault medical exam, just like any other sexual assault case. There is, however, an added difficulty in doing the ASAV exam in a date rape. The medical examination looks for abrasions, tearing, etc. consistent with a forced sexual penetration. Frequently, this evidence will not be present during a date rape scenario. This is because if the victim has been kissing or fondling the suspect prior to the actual rape, the female body will frequently prepare itself for intercourse. Then when the victim says, "no," but the suspect continues his advances, with the female body already prepared for intercourse, sometimes you will not find the vaginal trauma that you will find in a stranger rape.

Remember that you, the officer, are not responsible for the scenario that led up to the rape. If the victim was dancing naked in front of twenty people at a party and then states that one of them forced intercourse on her, then that is exactly how your report should read. Your job as an officer is to collect as much data as you can and then let the District Attorney and the court decide if it is a prosecutable case or not.

Sample Report Narrative: Date / Acquaintance Rape

On Thursday, 12-11-97 at 1400 hours, I met with the victim, 97-138 (Betty) at her apartment along with her sister, witness Nelson. Betty told me that she wanted to report that she had been the victim of an acquaintance rape that had occurred on Sunday evening, 12-09-97.

Betty said she works for an insurance company in a middle management position. She told me that on Sunday, 12-07-97, it had been arranged for her and some of her coworkers to meet with some customers for a champagne brunch. This meeting was to be "half business and half pleasure." There were to be eight to ten people present at the brunch, and it was tentatively arranged that Betty was to meet the suspect in this case, who was a customer from the client company. Although there was no official "blind date" set up between Betty and the suspect, there was an understanding that if she and the suspect were to become acquainted during the champagne brunch, it might lead to a dating relationship. Betty indicated that she has been divorced for two years and currently does not have a boyfriend.

Betty said she and her friends met Sunday at about 11:00 a.m. at the restaurant and engaged in the meeting/social function. Betty said that she met the suspect and they seemed to get along quite well. The brunch lasted for several hours. Betty said at about 4:00 p.m., the brunch ended, and she decided to drive to the suspect's nearby apartment to leave her car at his apartment while they went somewhere else for the rest of the day. Betty stated that after having parked her car in the suspect's apartment complex, she got into his car and they drove to the beach, where they walked and talked for several more hours. Ultimately, they went to dinner together and then went dancing at a nightclub.

Betty stated that during the entire time she was with the suspect, he was very polite and cordial and that they did drink through the champagne brunch and at dinner and while dancing. She stated that although she was feeling the effects of the alcohol, she was not drunk. Betty also stated that while dancing, she did kiss the suspect on the lips while on the dance floor.

Betty said that around 10:30 p.m. they returned to the suspect's apartment. While still sitting in his car parked in the parking lot area, she had given him her telephone number and asked him to call her later on in the week. Betty then said that she needed to use the restroom prior to driving home. She went up to the suspect's apartment to use his bathroom.

Betty stated that upon entering the suspect's apartment, he directed her toward the master bathroom, which was actually located inside the master bedroom. After using the restroom, she came back out into the bedroom area and saw that the suspect was now standing in the doorway and blocking her exit from the bedroom, wearing only his boxer shorts. The suspect said something to the effect of "The evening's not over yet." Betty responded by telling him that she was not desirous of having any sort of sexual contact with him, and asked if he would step aside so she could leave the apartment.

Betty stated the suspect's demeanor had completely changed at this time. She stated he had been gentlemanly throughout the entire day and evening, but now he appeared to be very agitated and angry. She stated she tried to force her way past him in the doorway, but he simply grabbed her by the shoulders and pushed her back into the room. When she again stepped toward the doorway to try to exit, he punched her twice in the face using his left fist. Being punched in the face caused a great deal of pain and she sat down on the bed while holding her hands to her face. The suspect then approached her, pushed her down on the bed, and told her that she was going to "suck my dick."

Betty said she was fearful that the suspect might continue to hit her. She added that he is much larger than she, and was still in a very angry and agitated state. When he exposed his erect penis from the opening of his boxer shorts, she did, in fact, orally copulate him.

Betty stated that when the suspect told her to remove her clothing, she complied, adding that her left eye was starting to swell closed and she was fearful that she would be struck again. She removed all of her clothing and lay down on the bed as instructed. The suspect then performed oral sex on her vaginal area and then had vaginal intercourse with her. After completing the vaginal intercourse, the suspect told her that she was free to leave. He added that what had happened was only "rough sex" and that she should not be concerned about it. He also told her that he would call her later on in the week to make arrangements to see her again.

Betty said she dressed herself, left the apartment and drove home. Once at home, she called her sister, witness Nelson, and asked her to come to her apartment to assist her. When Nelson arrived, Betty explained to her what had happened. At this time, Betty was holding an ice pack to her left eye. Betty was reluctant to go to the hospital and/or make a police report at that time. However, Nelson did take photographs of her face and eye, just in case she decided to make a report later on. This film has not yet been developed, and Betty said that she would make it available to detectives within the next day or two.

I noted there was still some discoloration to Betty's left eye. She had covered most of this discoloration with make-up. I asked her to remove the make-up from the eye so that the photographs could be taken of her injuries.

While the photographs were being taken, I spoke with witness Nelson. She told me that she had been called around midnight four nights before by her sister. The victim was upset and crying at the time and stated that something had happened to her, but she would not elaborate over the phone.

When Nelson arrived at Betty's apartment, she saw that her left eye was swollen closed and that she was crying. Betty then told her sister that she had met the suspect at a champagne brunch, had spent the day with him, but when she tried to leave his apartment, he had struck her in the face and forced her to have sex with him. Betty did not elaborate as to any of the details of the sexual assault itself to Nelson. Nelson stated that she spent the rest of the night with her sister, during which time Betty continued to cry and tremble when she would recall what happened to her. Nelson attempted to get her sister to call a rape crisis hot line that night and/or the police department, but Betty was afraid to do so.

Betty said the clothing she was wearing that night had not been laundered yet and was still in her dirty clothes hamper. I had a Crime Scene Investigator collect those items for evidence purposes.

SPOUSAL RAPE

Spousal rape usually is seen in two forms. The first is the ongoing sexual abuse of the spouse during the course of the marriage; the other is when the husband and wife have separated and the estranged husband comes back and rapes his estranged wife.

Ongoing Spousal Abuse

In this situation, you will have the basic abusive environment where the suspect/husband is routinely physically and emotionally abusing his wife. As a part of this ongoing belittling and abuse of the female, it is not unusual for the husband to continually force sexual acts with her in a way that is meant to degrade and humiliate her. It is difficult to prosecute these types of cases because the victim, in essence, is consenting to the sexual acts. In these types of relationships, the sexual assault is just one more weapon in the husband's arsenal to hurt and humiliate his wife.

The officer has to be sure that he is not judgmental of the victim when she reports having been subjected to perhaps years of sexual acts with the suspect, none of which she consented to, but which she never objected to either.

A part of your interview process should include a little bit of background history as to how the husband and wife met and if their relationship was ever "normal" in the beginning, and about what time it changed into this abnormal abusive relationship. The victim will normally relate an ongoing series of sexual assaults by the suspect/husband. You want to document the last time this happened in some detail. Normally, the last time there was a sexual assault, it happened just prior to the victim finally leaving the household and going to a women's shelter for protection. Since this is the most recent sexual assault, you will be in a position to collect physical evidence just as you would in any other rape scenario.

Sample Report Narrative: Ongoing Spousal Rape

On 8-12-97, at 1100 a.m., I met with victim 97-076 (Nancy) in the lobby of the police department. She was accompanied by a volunteer (Mary) from the Women's Transitional Living Center (WTLC). Mary told me that the victim, Nancy, had come to WTLC two nights ago after having been sexually assaulted by her husband. She stated that Nancy was now willing to make a police report about the sexual assault.

I took Nancy and Mary into a private interview room where I could speak with them. Nancy told me that she has been married to the suspect for eight and a half years. She told me that for the first five years of their relations, everything seemed normal. However, after the birth of their first child, the suspect seemed to change. She stated that he began to drink and became argumentative with her quite frequently. She said that occasionally, he would actually become physically assaultive, slapping her and sometimes kicking her. She said these physical assaults would occur perhaps once every four or five months.

Nancy stated that two months ago, she gave birth to their second child. She told me it was a difficult delivery and she has been under a doctor's care since the delivery. Because of this, she has not been able to return to work as soon as she did after the first pregnancy. She told me that not returning to work has caused some financial strain on the family, and because of this, the suspect has become more argumentative with her and become more physically abusive.

Nancy told me it had not been unusual during the last several years of their relationship for the suspect to want to end an argument by having sex with her. She told me that normally, after he had been very angry and enraged, he would tell her that he wanted to show her that "he loved her," and even though they were arguing, he would demand that she have intercourse with him. She told me that she would comply with his requests for sex because she knew that after having sex with him, he was not likely to continue the physical assault.

Nancy said that three days ago, in the morning hours, her husband decided not to go to work, stating that he was not feeling well. At about 9:00 a.m., Nancy had finished feeding their infant and put him down for a nap. After doing so, the suspect approached her and demanded that they have intercourse, stating that "it's been long enough" and added that he felt her internal injuries had healed sufficiently for them to have sex. Nancy tried to explain to her husband that she still had some sporadic vaginal bleeding from internal injuries and she did not think it would be safe to have sex at that time. This agitated the suspect, who slapped her once across the face, stating that he wanted to have intercourse with her.

Nancy stated that she complied with his request and disrobed and lay down on top of the bed. She stated that he had intercourse with her for a couple of minutes until she started to bleed. The bleeding angered the suspect even more and he slapped her twice more across the face.

The suspect then demanded that she take a shower with him. They got into the shower in the master bathroom and he began to wash her body. Nancy stated she was confused by the suspect's actions because it was not normal for him to show any sort of concern for her, nor do they normally bathe together.

During the bathing process, however, the suspect took a bar of soap and inserted it into her vaginal canal telling her he thought this would cleanse her body. The bar of soap became lodged inside her vaginal cavity and he was unable to retrieve it. Later that day, Nancy had to go to her doctor to have the soap removed from her vagina.

Barbara stated that later that evening she decided to leave her husband and took both children and went to the WTLC where she has been housed since that time. (Note:To protect spousal abuse victims and prevent their whereabouts being determined by the abuser, the locations of all shelters are secret.) Barbara indicated that she could be reached through her sister, as indicated on the face sheet of the police report.

I then called Dr. Smith who confirmed that the victim had come to him for removal of the soap from her vagina.

Estranged Husband

It is not unusual to see an estranged husband and wife be involved in a sexual assault situation. Because of the emotional turmoil involved in a separation or divorce situation, often the male becomes very angry and needs to act out his anger in some fashion. He sees the ex-wife as being the source of all of his bad feelings and emotions.

Men have the ability to take all of their emotions, be they helplessness, sadness, anxiety, and turn them all into anger and then project the anger toward what they perceive to be source of all of these feelings. They want to feel better (balance the emotional teeter-totter in their head) by making the victim feel worse than they do. Through this projection of their feelings into the victim, they will often come back to the family home and sexually assault the victim.

In these scenarios, you have the same sort of rape dynamics as in any other sexual assault. You have an approach of the suspect toward the victim; there is the initial contact, which might be under the guise of wanting to reconcile the relationship, or making some sort of support payments. Then you have the capture part of the assault, where the ex-husband actually captures her just like in a stranger rape scenario.

You then have the assault itself, followed by the post-assault behaviors in which the husband will often blame the victim for what took place. In this type of scenario, the husband frequently sees the wife as being his personal property that he can possess and use in any way that he sees fit, including the forced sexual act.

In this type of scenario, you document the sexual assault just like you would any other assault and interview the victim accordingly.

Sample Report Narrative: Estranged Husband Spousal Rape

On 2-6-98, I met with victim #98-36 (Jane) at the front desk of the police department. She stated that five days ago she had been raped by her estranged husband. I took her into an interview room to speak to her about the assault.

Jane said that she married the suspect four years ago. Within the last year, their relationship had deteriorated, and they had separated. Jane moved into an apartment by herself, which is where the crime occurred.

She said that Sunday afternoon, February 1st, she was lying by the swimming pool of her apartment complex when the suspect approached her on foot. The suspect told her that he wanted to talk about the divorce and the division of property. He said that he wanted to go into her apartment to discuss these matters.

Jane was fearful of him because it appeared that he had been drinking. She initially refused to go inside with him, but he told her that if she did not go inside with him, he would send copies of nude photographs of her to her family and friends. Jane told me that during their marriage the suspect had taken many sexually explicit photographs of her, some of them while posing with marital aids.

Jane said she was very interested in having these photos returned to her, so she agreed to go to the apartment with the suspect. Once inside, they began to argue and she asked the suspect to leave. She told him that she had to meet with some friends and needed to change clothes. She did this hoping that the suspect would leave so she could change. She entered her bedroom and removed her swimming suit at which time the suspect walked into the bedroom. They continued to argue while she was dressing. While Jane was still partially nude, the suspect demanded to know if she had a boyfriend or if she had been sexually active with anyone else. Jane told him that she had not been sexually active, but he did not believe her.

When she turned her back on him to step toward the closet, he grabbed her by the shoulders and threw her onto the bed. He then told her that she belonged to him. He then pulled the underwear off her lower body while sitting across her legs. She told me that she was afraid that he would hurt her by punching her in the face as he had two years prior when they had argued and he had been drinking.

The suspect took his pants off and she saw that he had an erection. He demanded that she have sex with him. He got on top of her and had intercourse for about three minutes. Jane said that she did not struggle with him at this time because she just wanted to get it over with, hoping he would not harm her. Prior to leaving the apartment, the suspect told her that if she reported the rape no one would believe her and he would deny it.

Jane stated she had since laundered the clothing and the bedding upon which the rape occurred. She delayed reporting the crime because she did not think anyone would believe her and she was still hopeful that the suspect would return the nude photos of her. She told me that last night she received a call from her mother telling her that the suspect had mailed several of these photographs to the mother and other family members. She decided to come to the police department to report the rape.

A rape examination was not done because of the time lapse between the rape and today's date.

SENILE / ELDERLY VICTIMS

This section is intended as a discussion about victims who are in retirement homes, nursing homes, or other types of care facilities. Because of their age, their medical problems and disabilities, they are very vulnerable to sexual assault. Also, as discussed earlier, they are seen as non-sexual, or asexual victims and are perfect targets for the type of offender that wants to assault this type of victim. Some sex offenders seek jobs as a night nurse or medical aid in a nursing home facility where they have access to countless numbers of victims who are perhaps nonverbal, or unable to report or resist any sort of sexual assault.

You, as a responding officer, need to obtain a lot of medical background from the doctors or nursing staff and the victim's family as a part of your investigation. You will have to understand exactly what types of physical and mental problems the victim has. This will give you an idea as to how she is able to relate what took place to you.

There is also the problem with the generation difference between you and the victim. You, as an officer, might have difficulty talking to someone who is older than your grandmother about a sexual issue. Also, the victim may have difficulty discussing the forced sexual act, as she came from a different time when such issues were not discussed at all. You may also have to identify body parts to be sure you and the victim are talking about the same thing. Since our language has grown and changed over the last several decades, you want to be sure that you and the victim are talking the same language when she talks about being forced into some sort of sexual act.

Because of vision problems, hearing problems, and all of the medical problems that accompany the aging process, the victim may not be able to identify the suspect in the usual fashion, such as showing her a photo lineup or even doing an in-person lineup.

Sometimes, this identification process is overcome by a witness who actually walked in on the assault as it was taking place. More often, it is accomplished by narrowing down the potential suspect pool circumstantially. You would do this by having one of the nurses who routinely checks on the victim, say on an hourly basis, indicate that the victim was clothed and was fine at midnight, but when she returned at 1:00 a.m., she found the victim to be upset, partially nude and bleeding. You then determine who had access to that victim, or who entered the room during that one-hour time frame, which would narrow down the possible suspect pool. Then the collection of physical evidence would become very important as far as using biological evidence, hairs and fibers to further identify the suspect.

Keeping all of this in mind, the actual interview of the victim should follow as closely as possible the interviewing techniques used for other sexual assault victims.

CHAPTER 5 INTERVIEWING AGES 18-80

Sample Report Narrative: Senile / Elderly Victim

On Saturday, 3-7-98, at 8:00 a.m., I received a radio call to respond to the Happy Hills Convalescent Hospital regarding a possible elder abuse and sexual battery. I spoke with Nurse Wilson who stated that she believed that one of the residents of the home had been assaulted. Wilson stated that at 3:00 a.m. this morning, she made her usual rounds and found that the victim was asleep and in good condition. At 7:00 a.m. while making her rounds, she observed a long cut across the victim's forehead and saw that her nightgown had been pulled to the side exposing her breasts. The victim told Wilson "he violated me."

Wilson stated that the victim is 89 years old and suffers from multiple medical problems, including a loss of eyesight and hearing and suffers from short-term memory loss, along with a heart condition and other ailments for which she takes medications. Her primary physician is Dr. Ross, who is out of town and won't be back until Monday.

Paramedics were called to the scene to examine the cut. They stated it was severe enough to require transportation to the emergency room for the victim to be treated. Prior to going to the emergency room myself, I had the convalescent home's staff roll up the bedding and place it into a paper bag for me to take as evidence. I also requested that the staff prepare a list of all employees that were on duty between midnight and seven.

When I arrived at the emergency room, Dr. Davis had closed the head wound with ten stitches and told me that the cut was not made by a sharp object such as a knife but was more likely caused by her being struck in the head and cut with a ring on someone's finger. Dr. Davis also conducted a vaginal examination of the victim due to the possibility of her having been raped. He told me that her vaginal opening was quite small and would require the use of a pediatric vaginal speculum to do the exam.

I made arrangements for the victim to be transported by private ambulance to Martin Luther Hospital where the staff is more experienced in conducting sexual assault exams. I attempted to interview the victim, but due to her age and her mental state (senility), all she would say was, "he violated me." I was of the opinion that this meant that she had been raped.

At Martin Luther Hospital, Dr. Adams conducted an ASAV exam on the victim. He told me that the victim's bladder had actually fallen into the vaginal canal which is not unusual for a woman her age. Once he lifted the bladder, he found that she had a normal vaginal opening and saw multiple tears and abrasions that were consistent with her having been raped. He also collected what he believed to be seminal fluid from the back of the vaginal vault. I obtained the sexual assault kit from the doctor for evidence.

Since the victim has no relatives living in the area, the private ambulance returned the victim to the convalescent home. I also returned and obtained the list of employees and the guest/visitor's sign-in book that is normally kept at the front desk. Anyone visiting the facility is required to sign in prior to visiting any resident.

Prior to leaving the facility I called the Elder Abuse Registry and asked them to arrange for alternative living arrangements for the victim.

Conditional Exam / Interview

The law allows, under certain circumstances, for the victim of a crime to be interviewed outside of the courtroom and then that interview be used for courtroom purposes. The law requires the defense counsel be present during this interview and that the defense have an opportunity to cross-examine the victim. As long as these requirements are met, the interview of the victim outside of the courtroom can be introduced later on as evidence in the trial itself.

When dealing with the extremely elderly victims, it is often necessary to conduct such a conditional exam in order to obtain their statements in case they die prior to trial. The conditional exam is generally set up between the assigned detective and the District Attorney's Office. A judge, court reporter, defense attorney, and even the defendant will be brought to the victim's hospital room so that the questioning can take place at the time. The law requires that the conditional exam be conducted with the suspect's lawyer present. If the suspect has not been arrested yet, or even identified yet, then you cannot conduct the exam.

In this situation, you might consider videotaping your interview with the victim in the hopes that the District Attorney could argue later in court that since the victim has now passed away, your videotaped interview might be used in lieu of her testimony. I don't know of any court decision at this time that will allow that, but it at least would be one way of preserving the victim's testimony on the chance that she might die prior to going to court.

When you have a suspect who is operating inside a nursing home, you may have multiple victims. Since many of the victims will be aged or in ill health, and the possibility exists that they may not live long enough for the case to make it to court, the videotape may be your one hope of presenting corroborative evidence as to MO, as in a signature-type crime, or for sentencing or other legal issues.

Elderly victims are very vulnerable to sexual assault. To successfully prosecute these extremely difficult cases, the responding officer has to do a very thorough and in-depth investigation.

MENTALLY HANDICAPPED / RETARDED VICTIMS

There is an entirely different set of issues you may run into when dealing with an adult who has some severe mental disabilities or retardation. These people grow up in an entirely different environment than the rest of society and, as a result, their culture is actually different than yours or mine. They have grown up in a culture where they have been taught to be compliant. Also, their lives are very structured. They have people who help them get up in the morning, help them clean themselves, bathe themselves, dress themselves, help them eat, take them to their daily activities, feed them lunch, help them in their afternoon activities, and then bring them back to their residence where they again help them clean, bathe, and prepare for bed. Almost every minute of the day is scheduled for them. Their entire schooling/training has been to get them to accept the routine and to do the routine as best as their abilities allow them to do. Because of this, they have been rewarded for being compliant and for doing whatever their caretakers require them to do.

This "learned compliance" makes them very vulnerable victims. Depending on which study you want to review, handicapped adults are victimized at a rate of two to ten times more frequently than non-handicapped adults.

Background Information

Prior to approaching an interview with such a person, you need to obtain as much medical background about them as possible. If you can, locate their primary care provider and ask this person what you can expect from the victim as far as language levels and their ability to interact with you. This will give you a great deal of insight as to how to approach the victim. If you can have this primary care provider assist you in the interview of the victim, that would be of great benefit.

Don't assume that because the victim has an IQ or the "mental age" of a five-year-old, that the victim wants to be talked to as you would talk to a five-year-old. Depending on the victim's life experiences, they may have some abilities similar to an adult and they would generally prefer to be talked to on that level. This is the type of information you can obtain from the primary care provider.

Interview: Mentally Handicapped / Retarded Victim

When talking to this type of victim, you want to be sure you maintain a comfortable distance from them physically. This is a distance that makes the victim comfortable talking to you. Unlike dealing with a small child, where you want to sit close to them so you can interact with them and touch them, you want to do just the opposite with someone in this category. It is quite possible that the person will object to being touched or having you too close to them and they might violently react to any such invasion of their "space."

It may take several separate contacts with the victim until they feel comfortable enough to talk to you at all, let alone talk about the sexual assault. Once you do establish a rapport with them, you have to be sure you are speaking the same language. Identifying body parts and terminology is very important. Most of these people have been taught human anatomy and have proper names for their body parts. This has been done for hygiene reasons and to teach them about sexuality, in general. It is not unusual for someone who you might consider to be retarded to use proper body names for their genitals.

The severely handicapped/retarded have many care providers in contact with them throughout the week. As a result, the list of potential suspects could be quite lengthy.

Interviewing someone with a physical or mental handicap requires a lot of patience on the part of the officer. There are variations within the abilities that each of these people have, so don't assume that because someone is retarded that they can't give you an accurate description of what took place. The difficulty comes in being able to understand their speech, and being sure that you are speaking the same language they are. The primary care provider for such a person should be consulted during the course of the interview to be sure that you are understanding what the victim is saying.

If you come into a care facility where one patient is pregnant, you should suggest to the staff of the nursing home that they check the other female patients for pregnancy and sexually transmitted diseases.

CHAPTER 5 — INTERVIEWING AGES 18-80

Sample Report Narrative: Mentally Handicapped / Retarded Victim Report

On 9-15-97 at 1515 hours, I met with the reporting party, Natalie Johnson, at Canyon Valley High School. Canyon has a student body population that includes students that are in Special Education or have special needs, such as being handicapped or retarded. Mrs. Johnson works within that part of the campus that deals with these special needs children.

Mrs. Johnson told me she was concerned about victim 97-1101 (Alice). Alice is a seventeen-year-old female who has a mental capability of a six-to-seven-year-old. Mrs. Johnson said that earlier today, Alice began to complain that her stepfather was fondling her breasts and making her feel uncomfortable every time she was with him. Mrs. Johnson added that Alice lives in a residential care facility during the week which transports her to Canyon Valley High School each day for her daily activities. On weekends, she returns home to live with her biological mother and stepfather.

Mrs. Johnson stated that Alice is a rather passive teenager who is often shy around strangers. She suggested that I not attempt to get too close to Alice for fear that she might run away. She also stated that when Alice starts to like somebody, it is not unusual for her to grab them in a "bear hug" and not let go for several minutes. Because of this behavior, Mrs. Johnson suggested that during my initial contacts with her, I sit across the desk from her in order to not invade her "space." Mrs. Johnson added that Alice has a rather complete vocabulary, but she speaks with a lisp and also drools when speaking. This makes it rather difficult to understand her at times. She suggested that I speak very slowly to Alice and then listen very carefully to what she was saying. Although Alice has some mental deficits, she can understand simple questions and can carry on a normal conversation.

Alice was brought into Mrs. Johnson's office and Mrs. Johnson was present during the interview. I was introduced to Alice and sat at a table with her. In order to establish a rapport with Alice, I began to draw a stick figure of a female on some notebook paper I had. I then asked Alice if she wanted to help me complete the drawing and she then drew some clothing onto the stick figure. Since Mrs. Johnson told me that Alice had been taught the proper names for both male and female anatomy, I did not see a need to identify body parts during this initial process. However, this developed a rapport between Alice and me, which allowed me to begin to ask if anything "bad" ever happened to her when she returned home on weekends.

Alice told me that sometimes her stepfather makes her walk around the house without her "top" on. She also stated there were times when he had actually come up behind her and placed his arms around her, putting his hands on both of her breasts when she was not wearing clothes. She told me that this happened both in the bathroom and the bedroom.

I asked Alice if she could remember what happened during the first incident . She said that her stepfather had initially started by rubbing her back, which made her feel good. She went on to state that after rubbing her back, he reached around and initially squeezed her breasts over her clothing. She said that after that, he would begin to squeeze her breasts both over and under her clothing. Alice was unable to give any sort of time frame as to when this first started to happen, nor could she give me an idea as to the number of times it occurred.

Alice said that these touching incidents made her "feel sad." She also added that she was afraid to tell her mother about what was happening because she knows that her mother loves the suspect.

Nothing further was gained from the interview with Alice.

Mrs. Johnson stated she was going to contact Alice's social worker and make arrangements to be sure that Alice was safe the next time she returned home for the weekend.

SATANIC CULTS

The mere existence of Satanic cults is of no interest to law enforcement unless they are involved in illegal activities. The only time they are of interest to the sex crime investigator is when individuals allege they have been sexually victimized as part of cult activities or the cult is using minors for sexual purposes during their activities. There have also been claims that cult members have been "baby breeders" and that these babies were conceived specifically for the purpose of being sacrificed during satanic activities.

Obviously, reports of mass homicides of infants by any organized group are very serious accusations. Many such crimes have been investigated by agencies, including the FBI, and to my knowledge, none of the claims were able to be proven. Occasionally, you will encounter a victim who claims to have either witnessed such satanic homicides or have been the victim of some sort of sexual assault by one or more members of the cult.

Interviewing someone who claims to be a victim of a crime resulting from ritual activity is relatively easy. From my experience, the best way to interview someone like this is simply to allow them to tell their story. These individuals are more than willing to tell their story to *anyone* who will listen. Many of them have ended up on the television talk show circuit, explaining about their victimization and the crimes they had witnessed.

Once they have finished telling you their story, you can ask them about specific details of the events that, if they actually occurred, would be easy to recall. There are key areas upon which to focus when asking about the specific details.

You first want to *ask about the location where the satanic acts took place.* Some of the more common responses will be motel rooms, churches that are closed for renovation, and remote, outdoor locations in the open desert or mountains. Usually, you will be given very vague recollections of the locations themselves.

With regard to motel rooms, often the victim will describe a room that is, in actuality, too small for all of the described activity to have occurred. When it comes to renovated churches, very rarely can the victims actually identify the location. The same holds true for outdoor locations; they cannot find them. It has been my experience that these types of victims cannot direct you back to the scene of the cult activity that holds any evidence that such an event took place.

Ask the victim *whether or not they suffer from Multiple Personality Disorder and, if so, what type of treatment or medication are they taking.* Frequently, you will find that they are in a group therapy situation, hearing similar stories from other members of the support group and the victim's statements would possibly be considered cross-contaminated.

A common theory regarding the lack of identifiable suspects and locations is that within one of the personalities, the entire cult and related activity exists and is acted out, as opposed to actually occurring "outside," in reality. I can neither support this theory, or refute that statement, since an in-depth discussion of Multiple Personality Disorder is not germane to this text.

Another key question for the reporting party is *to name the identities and occupations of the other members of the cult.* Typically, you will be told that some are law enforcement personnel, members of the clergy and sometimes a local mortician. These professional members serve several purposes. Believing some police officers are cult members, victims have been reluctant to come forward to law enforcement for fear that they would be speaking to another cult member and that any investigation could be derailed by members of the cult who are also law enforcement officers. According to the victim, the clergy members supply the locations for the satanic activities to take place as well as use their position in churches to recruit additional cult members. According to the reporting party, the local mortician has the responsibility of disposing of the bodies that have been sacrificed during the satanic gathering.

While questioning the victim about associated details concerning the event, try to focus in on the mortician angle. Most people have very limited knowledge about morticians, so their descriptions of a mortician's activities will be very vague at best. Some of the more common descriptions of the mortician's participation is that he brings a portable crematorium to the satanic activity location and after "the babies are murdered," they are disposed of in the portable crematorium. You should ask for as detailed a description as possible of this portable crematorium. You may also want to ask how the local mortician has the portable crematorium registered with the Department of Motor Vehicles. Is it (a) a recreational vehicle, (b) a sport utility vehicle, (c) a commercial vehicle, or (d) none of the above since there is no such thing.

The amount of heat necessary to cremate the human body is tremendous. To my knowledge, there is no way to adequately insulate any sort of portable/mobile vehicle that could actually sustain such heat. Once the body is cremated, the bones have to be pulverized in order to properly dispose of them. Is the vehicle a combination incinerator and crusher? I think not.

Inquire of the victim if she believes she has been programmed by members of the cult. I have been told that victims were programmed to participate in the satanic activities by way of a post-hypnotic suggestion and other mind controlling methods used by cults. One 38-year-old victim told me that as a child, cult members had used the touch tone phone sounds to preprogram her. Now, as an adult, when she heard these tones on her phone, she would go into a "zombie-like" state, then leave her home and join the cult for the evening's activity, leaving with no memory of what had transpired due to a post-hypnotic suggestion. The problem with her revelation however, was that when this childhood programming (using the touch tone phone to trigger her behavior) supposedly took place, it would have happened at a time when touch tones had not yet been introduced.

Usually a recounting of the crime and behavior will contain a statement from the reporting party about being controlled by "supernatural powers." According to what I have been told, cult members use some form of mental telepathy to force the victim to go to a location, participate in satanic rituals (that normally include unwanted sexual activity between the victim and cult members), as well as occasionally causing the victim to levitate. Some have reported that the mind control is strong enough to block the victim's memory as to where and what events took place during the cult activity.

One of the last things you should solicit from the victim is past addresses. This will allow background information to be obtained to see if there have been similar reports made by that victim in other cities. Since many of these victims are tenacious in their reports to law enforcement, wanting something done about a crime they truly believe happened, it is necessary to document their statements as thoroughly as possible.

The steps toward proving or disproving an allegation of cult rape are exactly the same as in any other rape complaint. The purpose of your investigation, in this case, is *not* to disprove the statements made by the victim; you are asking questions designed to solicit the truth. Once the truth is discovered, it will automatically point toward a legitimate crime, or a fictitious one.

UNLAWFUL INTERCOURSE

California law has been changed so as to be "gender neutral." As a result, anyone, male or female, who has sexual intercourse with someone under the age of 18, be they male or female, is in violation of the law.

Generally speaking, these cases involve an underage female having sex with an older boyfriend. Frequently, the girl's parents find out about this by reading her diary or they discover that the daughter is pregnant, and they want to press criminal charges against the boyfriend. The parents are not allowed by law to press charges against anybody. Pressing charges is something that the District Attorney's Office does. Also, since hearsay in this issue is not admissible, the reading of the child's diary, or any spontaneous statements made by the child, do not constitute the elements of a crime.

In this type of situation, you need the victim to actually come forward and talk about having sexual intercourse with her boyfriend, that it occurred within your county, and that it occurred within the statute of limitations.

If you have a victim who is willing to do this, the interview process with her is very simple. All you have to do is establish a general time frame as to when the intercourse took place, that it was consensual in nature, that it was actual vaginal intercourse, *and* that the suspect knew that she was under age. The age issue is normally satisfied by the victim having told the suspect how old she is, by his having picked her up at a junior high school on several occasions, or by his attending her 15th birthday party, or by some other such means.

There is no reason to go into any great detail as to the actual sexual acts themselves. If the minor can indicate she was having vaginal intercourse with the suspect twice a week, every week for the past two months, and that it occurred at his house after school, then that is normally sufficient to fulfill the elements of a crime.

In these types of cases, it is also very easy to get the suspect to confess to having intercourse with the girl. Normally, if they are in a boyfriend-girlfriend relationship, he will be somewhat reluctant at first, but ultimately he will admit to being involved in that relationship and that it got "carried away" to where they were having intercourse, but that it was consensual in nature. Once you have those elements identified, that's really all you need to prosecute the suspect criminally.

Sample Report Narrative: Unlawful Intercourse

On 9-1-97 at 1600 hours, I met the victim's mother at her residence. The mother said that she had read the victim's diary and learned that she had been involved in a sexual relationship with her 25-year-old-boyfriend. The victim is fourteen years of age.

I interviewed the victim, who told me that about four months ago, she was introduced to the suspect via mutual friends. They struck up a friendship and, ultimately, a dating relationship.

The victim said that for the last two months, every Friday after school, she has been picked up at school by the suspect. They would then drive to his home since his parents were not at home on Friday afternoons. The victim told me that they would engage in consensual vaginal intercourse, usually twice each afternoon, at the suspect's home, in his bedroom. The victim stated that during these acts of consensual intercourse, she never used any sort of birth control or "protection." She added that she feels she might be pregnant at this time, as she is three weeks overdue in having her period. She added that she has told the suspect that she might be pregnant, and he indicated that he wants to help her raise the baby if she is, in fact, pregnant.

I telephoned the suspect from the victim's home. He identified himself by full name, birth date, address, and driver's license number. At first, he was reluctant to talk about his sexual relationship with the victim. However, I told him that the victim was possibly pregnant, and genetic testing of the infant would identify that he was the father. He then told me that he had, in fact, been involved in a consensual sexual relationship with the victim.

The suspect said that every Friday afternoon, for the last couple of months, he would pick the victim up at school, drive her to his home where they would engage in consensual intercourse in his bedroom. He added that he knew the victim was underage, but felt that it was okay to have sex with her because they were in love with each other.

TO TAPE OR NOT TO TAPE

Throughout this text, I have talked about the pros and cons of taping conversations. It may seem from the generalities made in this handbook that I am totally against tape-recording interviews; this is not the case. I am against routinely tape-recording conversations without having any understanding as to why it's being done. As I have said many times, the law does not require law enforcement to tape record anybody. Obviously, there are many instances when tape-recording someone is of great value. Suspect interviews would be one of these exceptions, as would reluctant witnesses or anyone who you think would change their story at a later date. Also, if you get that "gut feeling," or instinct that you need to tape-record somebody, then by all means, do so.

There have been times when I have been in court and questioned by the defense attorney as to why I did not tape-record a victim or a witness. The response to that question is, "There are several reasons why I did not." If the attorney inquires further as to what those reasons are, the answer should be:

1. "First of all, there is nothing in law that requires me to tape record anybody."

2. "Re-interviewing a child for the sole purpose of taping, violates the concept of limiting the number of interviews to reduce trauma to the child."

3. "I know that the rule of court is that any interviews that are tape-recorded have to be transcribed in order to be introduced into evidence, and transcribing an interview is a very time-consuming and costly process. It is the informal policy of my agency and me to not routinely tape-record people because transcribing those tapes is very labor intensive."

4. "It is my personal policy to only tape-record those individuals who I think might change their stories at a later date. My experience has been that suspects routinely do this, especially after they have talked with their defense lawyer, who may have suggested that they come up with a different version as to what actually transpired. Also, there are situations where family members might change their story for one reason or another, or in drug-related crimes such as homicide, where this type of witness routinely changes his story because of the subculture in which they live.

5. "I also might decide to tape-record someone if I had a *gut feeling* that there was a need to do that for some reason. In this particular case, since none of these elements existed, I decided not to tape-record my interview with the victim."

WHEN THE VICTIM WON'T TALK

It would be irresponsible of us to not tell you of those situations where, in spite of glaring evidence, a victim will not disclose to you, or will adamantly deny that anything took place. This has happened on numerous occasions, and in spite of eyewitness accounts, I have had victims who will not, for whatever reasons, tell you what happened to them.

I believe it is far better to accept that reluctance at the first contact rather than have five interviews where the victim says "nothing happened," then on the sixth, because of trust building or finally being tired of the victimization, they decide to tell you of their plight. You can be assured that a defense attorney can create a great deal of "reasonable doubt" about the validity of this victim's testimony by calling into evidence the first five interviews where they denied the crime.

As harsh as it sounds, our advice is to simply walk away, close the file, and go on to a victim who wants help. Protect the ones you can—the ones who are ready to be protected. The rest, unfortunately, may stay victims. Taking this approach always leaves the door open for a victim who may, at some future point, determine that they want to do something about the crime committed against them. Opening files is much easier than facing an experienced defense attorney with countless "nothing happened" interview reports that exonerate his client or would at least establish doubt.

While I may receive some criticism for this "walk away if they won't talk" position, I feel it is in the best interest of the victim to do so. I would rather take the knocks than see the victims experience them in court!

FEMALE ANATOMY

Over the last several years, there has been an increase in the technology used in the performance of the actual pelvic exam of a rape victim. Specifically, the use of a colposcope to help in the examination that leads to a lot more physical findings of force and trauma than was ever found in the past. Also, there are now nurse practitioners and doctors who specialize in this type of examination, who actually know what to look for and, as a result, the physical findings are more dramatic than they have been in the past.

During consensual intercourse, the female body goes through several anatomic changes in order to allow for vaginal penetration and then to trap the seminal fluid in the back of the vaginal vault in order to assist in conception. In a non-consenting act of intercourse, this body preparation does not take place. An experienced medical practitioner can find blunt force type of trauma and irritation/friction type injuries to the inside of the vaginal canal. Tearing to the posterior fourchette, and even bruising to the cervix itself, is not unusual evidence to be found during a properly conducted medical examination. The tissues inside the vagina are similar in consistency to the inside of a mouth or a cheek. These tissues are easily damaged during the forced sexual assault. They also heal quickly.

With the aid of the colposcope, which is basically an optical viewing device used to look inside the vaginal vault, the doctor can actually see the small, microscopic tearing inside the vaginal area that is consistent with forced intercourse. With the aid of a purple dye (toluidine blue) which adheres to the cell membranes that have been damaged by the friction of the intercourse, it is also quite easy to see that the vaginal area has, in fact, been damaged by this non-consensual sex.

The colposcope has the ability to photograph the internal injuries that the female has received. Quite often, these internal injuries are the only physical evidence you will find to support the victim's statement about a non-consensual sexual act.

If the ASAV reports states "No Findings" or "Within Normal Limits (WNL)" that doesn't mean the victim was not raped. The lack of injuries in healthy, sexually active women, is also common.

TEAMING OFFICERS AND ADVOCATES

The officer and the advocate have two very different roles, both designed to accomplish the same end; prosecution of the suspect and restoring the victim to a healthy life.

The advocate as used in this text is *not* the social worker or child protective services worker who might accompany the officer at the time of the initial interview. The advocate is a person from the county victim witness program, or the volunteer from CASA (Court Appointed Special Advocates), or the local nonprofit agency individual that is willing to help.

The advocate usually enters the case *after* the initial interview. Depending on their agency's protocol, they may be limited to entering the case only after it has been filed with the District Attorney's office. In situations involving rape, they will come out twenty fours a day, seven days a week, upon request from the police, usually meeting the officer at the hospital at the time that the sexual assault exam is being done.

The nonprofit organization advocate will enter whenever requested to do so, whether the case has been filed or not. Sometimes, they are the originator of the information that leads to a case. Since advocates from nonprofit agencies are *not* tied to county protocols, they have more latitude in what they can or will do.

The officer and the advocate must always keep in mind that the advocate is there to assist, *not take over the police investigation, collect evidence or do the interview.* Initially, the advocate should be given an outline of the case at hand, which would contain all of the necessary information they need to be effective. After that, any investigative information, new allegations, facts, incidents, or other information should flow from the advocate *to the officer*. It is important that the victim knows that the advocate is providing this new information to the officer in order to strengthen the case. This way the victim does not feel betrayed by the advocate.

Avoiding full disclosure of all details of the case to the advocate preserves the integrity of the case and prevents the advocate from being put in an awkward situation in the future. Never put the advocate in a position where they know more about the case than they should. This might place them under suspicion if there is a leak to the victim, suspect or press.

REMEMBER—THE OBJECTIVE OF ANY INTERVIEW IS TO GAIN INFORMATION, NOT GIVE IT OUT!! In addition to providing information to an officer, the advocate's job is to assist with the victim's psychological needs and to explain general procedures and protocols. With that in mind, the advocate does not need, nor usually want, all of the microscopic details that simply muddy their relationship with the victim.

Chapter 6

GETTING IT ALL

I've spent a lot of time trying to teach the readers how to go about "getting it all", among other things. But now is the time to tell you that this is a lofty and therefore unattainable goal. Perhaps I should have been telling you how to get as close to this goal as is realistically possible. An example might explain it best.

Suppose that your best friend took a month long vacation to Europe and toured several countries during a nonstop attempt to see the entire continent. Upon his return the two of you get together for lunch and you ask your friend to tell you "everything" about his trip. Your friend then talks for more than an hour about "everything" that happened.

Two weeks later you have lunch again and this time your friend tells you additional facts about his trip. Two weeks later, at another lunch, the same thing happens. Does this mean that your friend lied to you during your first lunch? I think not. Instead he just added some stories that he hadn't thought of the first time or he simply didn't have time to "tell everything" during the first lunch. In reality you will never hear about everything that happened during that month.

Now consider a child who was molested three or four times a week, every week for several years. Are we ever going to be able to GET IT ALL? Again, I think not.

If at some future date a defense attorney asks you a series of questions such as "Have you received training in how to interview witnesses?" "Does that training teach you how to get ALL the facts?" And "Are you trained to write all of those facts down in your police report?" (I think you can see where I'm going with this.)

If you find yourself in such a situation, remind the District Attorney of the hypothetical trip to Europe and see if the D.A. can find a way to use that story to rehabilitate you as a witness and bring a very important point home to the jury.

PART II:
INTERVIEWING SEXUALLY MOTIVATED OFFENDERS

Chapter 7

CASE SELECTION

DID YOU EVER WONDER?

When investigating sexually motivated crimes have you ever said to yourself:

- *This case stinks, but I don't know why.*
- *Why did the suspect do that?*
- *What is the victim really saying?*
- *How can I convince my sergeant to let me drop this case and work on a good one?*
- *How can I convince my sergeant to give me the help I need to work this case when he thinks it stinks and I don't?*
- *I know this suspect wants to talk to me, but I can't quite get him there.*
- *He molested a kid, so he has to be a pedophile, right?*
- *The DNA must be wrong. How can they match a case involving an 8 year-old molestation victim to a rape-murder of a 75 year-old woman?*
- *How do I make all the different definitions of sex offender's work for me in my daily case load?*
- *How do I use all this behavioral data against the suspect during the interview?*

I've asked myself these and other questions hundreds of times, only to discover that it's really not that difficult. What you need to do is back away from all the complex definitions and psychological mumbo jumbo that's made it too hard to work with, and start looking at it in a more generalized form.

CHAPTER 7 — CASE SELECTION

As a cop, your job is to catch sex offenders. Let some one else cure them. So you really don't need to know a long list of behavioral characteristics for an even longer list of sex offenders. What you need is to understand suspect behavior as it relates to your interviewing needs. And I'm referring to both victim and suspect interviewing.

When you start looking at the suspect behavior in broader rather than specific terms then you will start to add a behavioral component to your interviews and case development in addition to corpus, physical evidence and witness statements. This will give you an edge when interviewing sex offenders and answer the questions at the beginning of the chapter.

Most crimes and criminals are motivated by money or revenge. Sex offenders are motivated by a need to "feel good". Be it sucking on toes, the power and control of rape, or having sex with road kill; to them, sex is defined as anything that makes them feel good. Your job is not to figure out if rubbing soiled diapers all over oneself to gain an erection is the result of poor parenting or putting too much sugar on your Cheerios as a kid. Instead, your job is to see the behavior as being sexually motivated (makes him feel good) to, **a)** establish that the victim has been in the presence of a sex offender, **b)** to use this information to find the suspect, and **c)** get him to cop-out.

In the next few pages I will share some secrets about sex offenders that are so simple that you'll wonder why you didn't figure them out yourself. You will also begin to wonder why all those behavioral science guys made it so hard to understand. More important, you'll start to see how to add this information to your suspect interview strategy and increase your confession rate.

What I'm about to tell you is NOT a complete psychological profile of any type of sex offender. It IS a way to take your interviewing skills from the Junior College level to the Master Degree level, by teaching a simple, generalized, understanding of what sex offenders do and say.

Chapter 8

THEY DON'T LIKE EACH OTHER

It took me many years to realize that different types of sex offenders don't like each other! This simple statement is really quite profound. Knowing this gives you an interview strategy that you didn't have a minute ago.

Sex offenders see their own form of perversion as normal or, at the very least, they have found a way to rationalize it to where it becomes socially acceptable in their minds. However, they view other people's perversions or paraphilias, as strange, odd, abnormal, bizarre, and even criminal. So, if you were interviewing a power rapist who had assaulted a 12-year-old girl, your strategy would include:

"You know, my sergeant thinks you're one of those pedophiles. You know, the type that has a sexual preference for little kids. I think something else is going on here and I need you to help me in understanding it."

By contrasting the suspect to a type of offender that he doesn't like, you give him the opportunity to explain that he's really not that bad. At least he's not as bad as some other type of sex offender.

The "Sex Offender Diagram", (Fig 13), depicts the fundamental differences between different types of sex offenders. It is not meant to be a complete list of all types of people who commit sexually motivated crimes. But, it helps in gaining a generalized understanding of the different categories of sex offenders.

FIXATED (the first column), is also referred to as "Preferential Offenders".

The following are brief definitions of the different types of sex offenders.

Pedophile   Someone with a sexual *preference* for *pre-puberty* children.

There is a difference between *preference* and *performance*. It's commonly assumed that because a suspect is having sex with a child, that he must be a pedophile. True pedophilia is relatively rare in that the person must have a sexual *preference*, orientation or attraction to *pre-puberty* children. Contrast this to someone who can *perform* with a victim of *opportunity*.

Breaking into a house and molesting a child makes the suspect a rapist, not necessarily a pedophile. Next week the suspect may break in and rape an adult. Even in-family offenders, who have been molesting their kids for years, are more likely to be rapists than pedophiles.

An interesting item about true pedophiles is that they generally view children as just children, as opposed to distinguishing or exclusively molesting only one gender or the other. They are likely to molest both genders.

THEY DON'T LIKE EACH OTHER CHAPTER 8

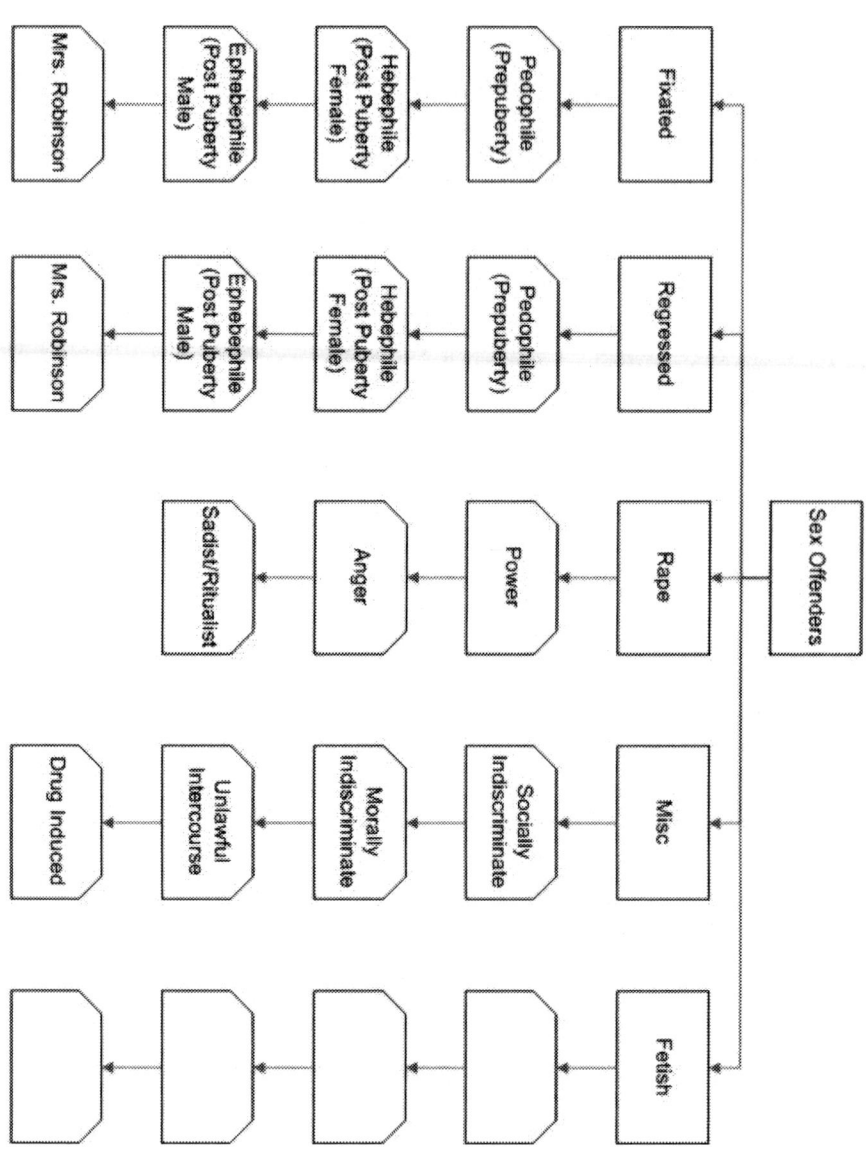

(Fig. 14) Sex Offender Chart
NOTE: There are hundreds of fetishes... too many to list.

Hebephile: Someone with a sexual *preference* for *post puberty females*.

Again, the trick is distinguishing between true preference and performance. These offenders by definition are selective as to gender. This is a male who at age 16 had a 14-year-old girlfriend. At age 26 he had a 14-year-old girlfriend; at 36 he had a 14-year-old girlfriend, and so on.

Phoebephile: Someone with a sexual *preference* for *post puberty males*.

Keep in mind the difference between a true sexual *preference* vs. being able to *perform* in diverse sexual situations. In my experience this type of offender is very active and will have multiple victims. He will have a parade of teenage boys in and out of his house at all hours. He will dress, talk and act like a teenager and make himself part of the teen scene.

Mrs. Robinson: A female with a sexual *preference* for *post puberty males*.

Named after the character in the movie, The Graduate, this offender has a sexual preference for under age boys. This is the school teacher having affairs with sixth grade students. Or the married mother of three who insists on driving the babysitter home on Friday night, stopping along the way to have sex in the back seat. There have been several news stories lately regarding this type of offender. They are more common than most people think. The duality in our society states that a boy is lucky to be broken in by an older woman but a girl is being taken advantage of by an older man.

I see a couple of different issues here. If the teenage boy is exposed to a level of sexual experience much higher than his peer group, how does he ever establish a normal relationship with a girl his own age? If a 12-year-old boy lies awake each night fearing that his step mother will come into his room and coerce him into sex, is that a passage into manhood or into terror? During a lecture I attended many years ago, the speaker theorized that many of the most violent serial killers and rapists had been molested by a woman when they were young.

All of the offenders in the Fixated group seek out long term relationships with children. They will seduce a child over a long period of time if necessary. They want to be accepted into the world of the child and view the sexual touching as proof of that acceptance. The offender sees himself as a peer to the child. He rationalizes that the love he shows the child far out weighs any harm that the sex might cause. He views sex with children as natural and normal. This is his sexual orientation. To the offender it is no different than being heterosexual or homosexual. The pedophile will want to have sex as often as those in heterosexual relationships. This can equate to hundreds of victims and thousands of molests during his life time.

Offenders in this category would never "hurt" a child. The idea of kidnapping and raping a child is foreign to them.

The next column refers to *REGRESSED* offenders, also called Situational offenders. The definition for those in this category is basically the same. It goes something like this:

Someone who normally has sexual partners that are age appropriate but when his life becomes conflicted, he seeks out underage relationships.

This offender may molest pre puberty or post puberty children. He tends to see the victim's has being older than their actual age and as being the sexual aggressors. His sexual contacts with these children are relatively few in number and occur during a brief time period. During the time frame of the molestations he will also continue having sex with age appropriate partners. He doesn't develop a long term relationship with his victims nor does he seduce them over time.

This is the nice uncle who has been babysitting his nieces since they were little with no hint of a problem. But when he finds himself going through a divorce, loses his home and job, and his car gets repossessed, he becomes emotionally unbalanced and molests the girls; usually a few times during a short time frame.

This type of offender can regress several times during his life.

It's my opinion that this category doesn't really exist. As you will see in a moment, the definition of a power rapist is almost identical to that of the regressed offender. From an interviewing point of view, regressed and rapist are the same.

The center column, *RAPE*, is what I like to refer to as the *power and control* offenders. I would strongly recommend that you read "Men Who Rape" by Dr. Nicholas Groth. His insightful work lays a foundation for an in depth understanding of rapist and other sex offenders. I will not try to repeat his work here. Instead, some brief definitions for the purpose of interviewing this type of sex offender will suffice.

Power rapist: This individual uses just *enough force to capture* the victim. During the initial phases of the assault, he is in a *heightened state of anxiety*. Once capture is complete, his anxiety level is reduced and he will start to act out the fantasy he has been re-playing in his mind over and over for an extended length of time. This results in a dialogue between the suspect and victim that is very instructional and inquisitive in nature.

There are a couple of sub categories of Power Rapists. Some seek approval, others reassurance. The important elements to remember when interviewing a rapist are:

- enough force to capture
- anxiety
- instructional
- inquisitive

These elements will be explored in some up coming examples.

Anger rapist: The anger rapist uses an *excessive amount of force* to capture the victim. His mental state is one of *extreme frustration and violence* and the actual sexual assault is simply one more mechanism for hurting or injuring the victim, just like punching or kicking. His dialogue with the victim is more *derogatory and degrading.*

Sexual sadist/ritualistic: The sexual sadist actually becomes sexually aroused by watching the suffering on the face of the victim. Any injuries, physical or psychological, are all done with the intent of creating this look of fear which, in turn, sexually arouses him. These individuals are relatively rare and law enforcement usually encounters them during the course of a homicide investigation.

Think of a rapist as having an emotional balance beam or scale inside is head. When the beam is level, he's stable and not acting out sexually. As the beam starts to tilt, or his life becomes conflicted, he begins to fantasize about getting even. For him, getting even has nothing to do with confronting the source of his problems.

The rapist will imagine assaulting a woman at random. This usually balances the scale and he stabilizes. If the beam tilts even more he will begin to act out on the fantasy. He may put together a rape kit, gathering the tools needed to complete a rape. A mask, tape, gloves, condoms and a gun or knife are common ingredients for his kit. He may prowl the freeways looking for a woman driving alone and follow her for miles, fantasizing about how easy it would be to force her off the road and rape her. This too helps balance the emotional scale.

As the beam tilts even further he will peep and prowl, taking note of every open window and woman living alone. He may break into a home and simply stand over a woman as she sleeps. Depending on how far the beam has tilted, he may fondle her or masturbate as she sleeps. Being close to the actual assault gives the rapist the feeling of power and control he needs to balance his emotions.

When tilted far enough he will put the fantasy into play, follow the six phases of a sexual assault and complete the rape. He may need to rape several times before the beam is balanced. Once done, he goes dormant, perhaps for years.

There's an urban legend that tells of sex offenders becoming more violent with each attack. Like a flight of stairs, the offender steps to higher levels of violence with each assault. This is not the case. If the balance beam in his head tilts suddenly and drastically, his first assault may be very violent with subsequent attacks being less violent as the scale balances. The stair step myth comes from an old study which concluded that over time there will be a slight increase in violence from an offender's first rape to his last. This refers to an average of violence over time. Think more of a roller coaster effect with some rapes being very violent and others much less violent. Averaging out the roller coaster results in a slight increase of violence in the long run.

Another myth is that all sex offenders will progress from minor offenses to the most severe. This would literally mean that anyone who exposes himself in public will eventually become a serial rapist. Again, this isn't the case. Think of it in another way. A bank robber will also shoplift; but not all shoplifters will become bank robbers. In my experience, many sex offenders reach their level of acting out by their early twenties. They seem to find what "works" for them and stick with it. Maybe it's driving around naked with the dome light on so the folks in the SUV can see him masturbate, or pinching ladies bottoms in crowded elevators. They seem to find a way to balance the beam in their heads. Pushing to a higher level would require a big life stressor.

Think of sex offenses in time clusters. Imagine your city being "quiet" for a long time. Then you get three apparently random sex crimes in one month. One is a burglary rape of an adult female in the middle of the night. Another is the burglary in which the suspect gets into bed, naked, with a

6-year-old while asking if it's okay for him to be "here." The child slides out of bed and runs down the hall as the suspect stares and masturbates. The third is an indecent exposure in which the suspect jumps out of the bushes, naked, scaring two teenage girls while asking if they want to watch him masturbate.

This could be the work of three separate suspects or perhaps only one. Remember that rapist look for victims of opportunity, so the age of these three victims is meaningless. I would want to re-interview all three victims, looking for the six phases of the assault and the dialogue during the capture and assault phases. The dialogue may connect the crimes. I would also send any DNA samples from these cases to the crime lab together. Science may make the connection for you.

I would also do one more thing. I'd talk with the burglary detectives. Residential burglars are first cousins to sex offenders. Especially the hot prowl burglar. You may discover a series of residential burglaries that started at the same time as the sex crimes.

In the next column, *MISCELLANEOUS*, I've listed four categories. The first two being Socially and Morally Indiscriminate. Identified by FBI agent Ken Lanning, these categories explain a large number of sex offenders that I've come across over the years. They are briefly defined as:

Socially Indiscriminate: This person engages in a wide range of sexual behaviors with consenting and non-consenting partners, both adult and children. This person understands that society views much of these activities as immoral, but he chooses to do them anyway. He finds ways to exploit individuals who are younger or weaker than himself.

Morally Indiscriminate: This person engages in a wide range of sexual behaviors with consenting and non-consenting partners, both adult and children. He has a complete lack of moral understanding of what society considers being right and wrong. The indiscriminate types do not have an associated rape fantasy. They offend because they simply do not care - think they can get away with it, or both.

I like to think of these two groups as being kinky. These are the guys that are doing all kinds of sexual stuff. When you search warrant their homes you find a wide variety of sexual material, from toe sucking to cannibalism.

Many years ago I assisted in the serving of a search warrant at a home where we hoped to find several dismembered bodies. Instead, we discovered a small group of men engaging in a variety of sexual activities. They were experimenters. To them anything imaginable was sex. Be it hanging weights from their testicles, sticking pins through their penises, or cutting open their scrotums to look inside; to them there was a fine line between pain and pleasure. This particular group was careful to involve only adults in their "fun."

Unlawful Intercourse: This group usually involves sex between teenagers. I've included it here because under California law, and other states too, if one of the teens is too old and the other too young, there is a violation of law. Generally, the participants are not viewed as sex offenders. However, it is sometimes difficult to decide if the teens will grow up and continue with age appropriate partners, or will they be seeking sex with teenagers when they are in their 40's?

Drug Induced: This is the offender who's been on a three day meth high and has sex with his girlfriends little sister. I like to think of this as a separate category. From an interviewing point of view, it is easy to approach the suspect along the lines of "the drugs made you do it." They still go to prison, but they do so thinking they really are not sex offenders.

The last column, *FETISH,* refers to a never ending list of sexual attractions to inanimate objects or specific parts of the body. Paraphilia is another term for these behaviors. Experts in the field report that people often have more than one paraphilia at a time, with one being dominant and the others subordinate.

There are three levels or degrees of fetishes: mild, moderate and severe. Law enforcement usually encounters the severe variety. However, I'm sure you know of someone in your department with a mild or moderate fetish. Perhaps it's for women with long hair, big breasts, small feet or hairy armpits. Many men are known for their fetish. The most common fetish is High Heel shoes. Many pornographic films include scenes in which the women are only wearing high heels. I doubt they are shy about exposing their feet or that they have ugly toes. Instead, the adult film industry is catering to this fetish.

A partial list of fetishes include: Bondage, leather and lace, toe sucking, balloon popping, bestiality, sex with dead bodies (human), sex with road kill (non human), urinating, defecating, enemas (giving or receiving), infantilism, cross dressing, voyeurism, exhibitionism. There are hundreds, maybe even thousands more.

CHAPTER 8 — THEY DON'T LIKE EACH OTHER

Most of the fetishes are not illegal per say. Many are very embarrassing to the people who have them. In my city there is a man who becomes aroused from the smell and consistence of soiled diapers. When his urge for dirty diapers is out of control he'll spend half a day collecting soiled diapers from the trash bins behind pre schools. He'll even pursue trash trucks in order to rescue diapers before they are commingled with other trash. His favorite is the squishing of several soiled diapers at a time, feeling the soft contents inside and enjoying the odor. His fantasy is to fill a trash truck with dirty diapers and video the compacting of a thousand or more diapers at one time. To him this would be the ultimate release. At the same time he knows that his fetish is weird and socially unacceptable. Dating is difficult, if not impossible for him.

Occasionally a fetish results in criminal behavior. The following is such as example:

Several years ago there was a man living in my city who had a fetish for women's butts. His fetish had narrowed to the licking of their butts. He would go to the local department store, get down on all fours and sneak up behind unsuspecting shoppers and start licking their butts. Dropping his keys on the ground afforded him the opportunity to bend down, look up their dress and start licking.

Most of the time he would get slapped or kicked and then move on to another store. After a while the women were hitting him so hard that the recovery time was taking longer and longer. So he started licking teenagers butts, and later preteens. After several arrests, he focused on 8 and 9-year-old girls, perhaps thinking they could not identify him.

He was arrested for attempted kidnapping of an 8-year-old girl on roller skates, when he was trying to hold on to her hips and push his nose into her butt as she was trying to skate away. A couple of passers-by tackled and restrained him until the police arrived.

His last arrest involved a 4-year-old girl at the local discount store. He approached her from behind and patted her on the butt so lightly that she didn't feel it. However, another mom saw the touch and chased him out of the store. A thinking CSI officer took the little girls pants. The crime lab identified a semen stain transferred from his hand to the child's clothes. The DNA identified the semen stain as our suspect's.

During the interview with him, I played heavily on the idea that he wasn't "one of those pedophiles", but instead had a more understandable "problem". Using the "different types of sex offenders do not like each other" approach resulted in a successful interview.

The law does not make the above distinction. He was still a child molester and this was his third strike that resulted in a life term.

Chapter 9

THE FIVE TRADEMARKS OF A SUSPECT INTERVIEW

After interviewing hundreds of sex offenders, I discovered some fascinating personality traits. Once I understood them, it became the most dynamic interviewing tool at my disposal. When a sex offender talks about the case under investigation, he will do five things:

1) Diminish the severity of the event
2) Blame the victim to some degree
3) Attempt to control the interview
4) Never give you 100% of the information regarding what occurred
5) Never tell you about crimes that you don't already know about

Understanding these five personality traits gives the interviewer a tremendous advantage. The trick is to sit back, allow the suspect to talk, recognize what he is doing and encourage him to continue. If he wants to make you believe that he only fondled the little girl vs. having intercourse, let him say that. If he wants to say that the 5-year-old seduced him, that's fine too. I'll take a partial confession any day. Don't try to force every little bit of information out of him. Doing so makes him feel out of control and he'll regain control (of the interview) by deciding not to talk. Sex offenders have a need to exercise power over their environment, so let them. Recognize that to the offender, knowledge is power. If he has information that you want, then he has power over you. The interview trick is to let him prove that he has the power. Let him give you a taste of the information. Let him feel like he's in charge of dealing out the information one card at a time.

Once you understand this, aspect 3, 4 and 5 make perfect sense. In #3 the suspect will control the interview by giving out little pieces of information or by going off on a tangent. Your job is to pull the information out of him and bring him back on course.

Aspect #4 is also quite clear. If he gives you 100% of the information he has no more power.

Aspect #5 is the classic interviewing question of, "do you want to confess to anything else?" I always ask this question, hoping that some day a sex offender will offer up all of his past sins. My experience has been that they will not. For some reason, if you don't already know about it, they are not going to admit to it. I'm sure there are some power and control elements to this. It's very important that you keep a professional rapport with the suspect, even after he's told you "everything". There was a time in my career when at the end of an interview I would "get in the suspect's face", just to see how he would react. Generally, he would just stop talking. There have been a few times when, to my dismay, when I reviewed the interview tape I discovered the recorder had malfunctioned and the tape was blank. Or, a neighboring city calls me, wanting to interview the suspect for crimes in their city. This is when I wished that I had left the "interview door" open so I could talk with the suspect again.

The following examples will emphasize the importance of these 5 aspects.

#1 - DIMINISH THE SEVERITY

If you have a rape suspect that held a woman hostage for several hours and committed a variety of sexual acts to her, you know that he will never cop-out to every one of them. So don't try to get 100 %. Settle for 40%. If he wants to confess to the rape and oral copulation, but not the sodomy, that's fine. In fact, you may want to set the stage for such a diminished confession.

Tell him that all the facts and reports are not in yet and you need to get his side of what happened. If he gives you 40%, don't push for more. The reason is that "control" is his heroin. Once again, if you push him too hard, he will control the interview by not talking. So, let him "win" during the interview. If he feels like he is "getting away" with lying to you then he will want to continue to lie to you. The more you keep him talking the more of a confession you will get. You may get up to 60% or 70%. Any confession is usually enough to get the guy to plead guilty. So in my mind it's more important to keep him talking and let him think that he's smarter than you than to get in his face and cause the interview to shut down.

Another factor that feeds in to this concept of diminishing the severity is that rapists believe that the victim wanted to be raped. They find it hard to understand that the victim would report the rape or want the suspect to go to jail. During the interview this equates to them thinking that the victim didn't tell you everything that happened. So, when you accept the 40%-70% story he's giving you, this fuels the rape fantasy. He feels that it was okay to do the other sexual acts because she didn't tell you about them. When you tap into his fantasy, it's difficult for him not to talk.

Child molesters will not only diminish the type of sexual acts committed, but the number of times they molested a child as well. Always keep in mind that most child molesters are NOT pedophiles. Many are power rapists and need to be interviewed accordingly.

#2 - BLAME THE VICTIM

Sex offenders are great at rationalizing their behavior. Blaming the victim is the easiest way to do it. Offenders see consent in just about anything the victim does. So, if a girl dances with him at a night club he sees that as an invitation to rape her in the parking lot. Kissing him at a party means its okay to wait until she passes out on the sofa and then rape her. Going outside to smoke marijuana is tantamount to consent, even at knife point.

Child molesters like to believe that children want to know about sex and therefore the molester is only teaching them something that they are curious about. They are also good at blaming the parents. If mom and dad had been better parents then the child would not have been searching for the suspect, someone that the kid can confide in. This leads to a sharing or closeness that leads to sex.

If a molester is a pedophile, he sees sex with children as normal and a peer type of relationship. So, during the interview you would approach him that way.

Examples:

A male in his thirties kidnaps a 16-year-old girl off the street at gun point and drives her 10 miles to a remote and secluded area to rape her. Along the way he stops at every red light and never speeds. After arriving at the secluded area the girl states that she needs to urinate. He lets her get out of the car, she goes behind some bushes and urinates and returns to the car. He then rapes her for over an hour before driving her home. On the drive home he asks for her phone number and where she works. A couple of hours after the rape he calls her to see how she is doing.

When interviewing this suspect point out to him that the girl could have jumped out of the car during the drive to the rape scene and she could have run away when she got out of the car to urinate. She also could have given him a false phone number and lied to him about where she works. All of this plays into the suspect's rationale that all girls really want to be raped and had this girl not wanted "it" she could have escaped at any time. In this particular case I assumed that the gun was a BB gun or replica. I was playing the percentages with this one, by knowing that the Power Rapist doesn't want to hurt the victim and will only use enough force to capture her. So, an educated guess was that he would choose a weapon that could not hurt her, even accidentally. So, during the interview I offered the idea to him that he "didn't even have a real gun", which diminishes the severity of the assault and blames the victim in that she could have run away at any time, and he could not have stopped (shot) her.

In another case the suspect had kidnapped several women as they were getting out of their cars at apartment complexes. He would have them get back into their car and drive him to an ATM machine and have them withdraw $300. He would stay in the car as they walked up to the ATM, get the money and return to the car. He would then have them drive behind the bank, rape them and then have them drive back to their apartment complex. There are two great interview avenues in this one. The first is to get him to cop out to taking the money with no mention of the rape. Remember, he thinks that rape and consent is the same thing, so in his mind the girl would be mad about the money and not mention the rape. After he cops-out to the robbery you bring in the "sex" adding that she could have run away when she went to the ATM machine.

Keep in mind the third phase of a sexual assault. This is the Capture Phase in which the victim is psychologically captured by the suspect. She has accepted that she can not get away and is trying to "play along" with the suspect so he doesn't kill her. That's why she gets back into the car and/or doesn't try to escape. The suspect had learned this behavior during the course of his rapes, which tells us that he has done this before and is an experienced rapist.

Child molesters will blame in a slightly different way. When molesting young children the force to capture is replaced by a trick, promise or game. I interviewed a 50-year-old man for molesting three neighbor girls between the ages of 3-9 years. He had offered to watch them after school. One of the games he taught them was to dance the can-can in which they would pull up their dresses. It was a short process to get them to sit on his face so he could "blow air on them" as a form of tickling. He would also give them candy to hide on their bodies and he would have to "search" for the candy. During the interview you start off by understanding that he is NOT a pedophile. So, you tell him something like this:

> "I don't think you're one of those guys with a sexual preference for children. I think maybe the kids took the game playing too far and now you're in a big mess".

This diminishes the severity and blames the kids, and even mom, for not being home to watch them.

Remember, a true pedophile views sex with children as natural and normal and doesn't rationalize it away. He knows that society sees it as being "sick", but he does not. He will study all about pedophilia. He sees himself in a peer relationship with children and he would never hurt a child, and instead will develop a relationship or seduction process over time. He believes that the love he gives to the child out weighs any possible damage that the sexual touching might do. The easiest way to diminish the severity and blame the child at the same time is to tell him just that. I like to tell them, "I don't think you're the type of guy that would stand out side of the playground with a bag of candy and try to kidnap and rape a child. But if you don't tell me what really happened here, the Judge and jury might think just that. I'm thinking that this kid needed someone special in his/her life and you stepped in and the relationship grew into something sexual". It helps if you tilt your head to the side and have a "please help me to understand" look on your face.

To put this idea of blaming someone else into context, we as police officers have been doing it for a long time in other interviews. Think about the bank robber with a drug habit. You tell him that he had no choice but to rob the bank because of the drugs. If he capped off a couple of rounds while in the bank, well he didn't hit anyone and if he did, it was only a flesh wound. And if someone did die, well they were old and wouldn't have lived much longer anyway. We've played the "diminish and blame" game for years. The only change now is that the motivation for the crime is different, so we have to change gears to meet the suspect's behavior.

#3 - CONTROL THE INTERVIEW

Sex offenders love to go off on tangents, as well as turn the interview table around and interview you. When you "see" this happening, realize that you are in the presence of a sex offender. In other words, you probably have the right guy.

If they catch you in a lie or feel that you don't have the facts straight, they have already won. There is no need for them to confess because they are already in control.

Going back to the example of the suspect that kidnapped the girl then drove her ten miles to a secluded area to rape her. He was driving a white pick up truck he had "borrowed" from his work site. The problem I had when interviewing him was that I didn't know there were several white trucks at this site, and I assumed the one he used in the rape was the one he drove while on the job. This became a sticking point in the interview that I couldn't get around. So I stopped the interview for a couple of hours until I straightened out the truck issue and then talked with him again. Within a few minutes he started confessing to the rape and ultimately took me back to where he had first seen the girl, showed me the route he took to the rape site and where he had hidden some of the evidence. He wouldn't show me everything and would only cop out to raping her once instead of three times, but that was enough to get him to plead to a life term.

#4 - NEVER TELL 100 %

We've been touching on this one for awhile now, but with sex offenders it's a little more involved than with other criminals. Control is the sex offender's heroin and he is addicted to it. To have something that you want gives him power, and therefore control. If he tells you everything he knows, he has no more power, no more control. So, he will keep some things to himself. Think of the serial killer that confesses to ten murders but won't talk about the other two. Why? Because he still has something that you want, which gives him the feeling of still being in control.

The next logical question is "why would he talk at all?" It's really rather simple. To prove that he has the power he has to give you some of the information and withhold the rest. This means that it's your job to set up an interview strategy in which the suspect thinks that he can "win". Remember that winning to him means being in control. Since control is his addiction, he has to have it NOW. He can't wait a week, or a month… he needs it now.

I like to set up a "soft interview". This is where I'm not too sure of the facts and I need his help to clear up a few things. It also allows me to back away from an area where my facts are not accurate. I never start off with a posture that I know what happened and he might as well just cop out to it.

These guys love to manipulate. So let them. The more they talk, the better off you are. Remember the Colombo television series many years ago about the stumbling and bumbling detective who let people out smart him right up to the time they went to prison? That's the type of process I'm talking about, but not to that extreme. If you're too "stupid" the suspect probably won't talk to you. I've found that most sex offenders have big egos. So, I always introduce myself as the "lead detective" or the "head of the investigation". As the interview unfolds I like to add that I've been investigating sexually motivated crimes for many years, gone to all the classes, lecture to other detectives and anything else I can think of. You never want to be the "low man on the totem pole" detective or the new kid on the block. The sex offender needs to feel that he and the case are so important that the best and brightest were called out to talk to him.

Sex offenders, especially the power rapist, need to fuel their ego. They are intimidated by authority figures, yet they want to feel powerful themselves. This means that you have to balance the command presence posture that we normally convey with a softer, less threatening style. If the suspect knows that you are the "lead detective" called in to talk to him, that feeds his ego. Thinking he can manipulate you feeds his addiction for power and control.

Example:

I was teamed up with one of our homicide detectives working a rape-murder of a 50-year-old woman, who was also the town drunk. She had been stabbed about 70 times, strangled and had her back broken. Her body was found in a vacant field. A 19-year-old suspect was developed and we brought him in for interview. The homicide detective was interviewing the suspect like he was a killer. He was not at all successful. When it was my turn, I tried a softer approach. I talked to him like he was a sex offender who had accidentally killed.

I started by showing him a mug photo of the victim's last drunk in public arrest and implied that since she was the town drunk, she wasn't an important person. In his mind, this diminished the severity of the crime, and blamed her at the same time. Next I talked about how I "really needed to know" what happened so I could tell the judge and jury. Because I didn't think that he was really a killer, and that something else must have happened.

It was like a light went on in his head. He looked at me and said, "Well, you will probably identify my fingerprints in the mud next to her body, so I might as well tell you." He went on to say that he had met her at a party and agreed to buy her some beer afterwards. (To him this meant that she had consented to have sex with him.) When they went to the vacant lot to drink, he "came on to her", but she refused his advances. When he exposed himself to her, she laughed at the size of his penis, which enraged him. From that point on his story was rather vague. But he did admit to forcing "sex" with her and stabbing her one time with a small pair of scissors from her purse. He said he didn't know anything about her strangulation or broken back.

So, I had to decide to force the issue about the strangulation and broken back, or I could let him "win" that one and not try to get 100% of the facts concerning her death. I chose not to force the issue and instead asked him to show me where he discarded his bloody clothes and her purse. He was happy to take us to the clothing and the purse, and on the way, he took us back to the scene of the murder, giving us a brief overview of how it occurred.

#5 - NEVER TELL YOU ABOUT CRIMES THAT YOU DON'T ALREADY KNOW ABOUT

This is the classic interview fishing trip. Once the suspect has confessed to the crime you know about, you always want to ask about other crimes he may have committed. I'm hoping that some day a suspect will open up and tell me about a string of rape murders, but it hasn't happened yet. What I have learned to do is to leave the interview on friendly terms. Then if I do learn of a new crime, I can approach him again. When I first started interviewing sex offenders, I would try to "get in their face" at the end of an interview. My thinking was that I might force them into saying something new or perhaps get them to become angry so the jury could see who they really are. It never worked. Instead, they just stopped talking.

Closing on friendly terms leaves the door open for additional interviews, perhaps by a neighboring city. The offender can end up viewing me as the only person who understands him. Occasionally, when raising my right hand to be sworn in as a witness I've seen a suspect give me a friendly little wave back, much to the dismay of his attorney.

I would also strongly suggest that you do not lie to the suspect during the interview. Some detectives are very good at fabricating evidence or witnesses to the crime as a technique to get a confession. I'm not totally against it, but at the very least, use it as a last resort. Sex offenders are clever people and if they catch you in a lie, then they have achieved control over you. Since control is all they care about, they have "won" the interview and have no reason to confess.

An example of this was a kidnap/rape case of a young girl who one evening walked almost a mile from her home to a convenience store. On the way home she said that she was kidnapped at gun point from the store parking lot, driven a couple of miles away, raped and then pushed out of the car naked. She had been found nude, then taken to a hospital where the rape exam confirmed the sexual assault.

A suspect was developed and brought in for interview. The detective decided to fabricate a security video tape, showing the suspect's car in the stores parking lot, which when enhanced would show the suspect behind the wheel at the time of the kidnapping. It seemed like an easy enough lie, but the suspect knew that he had only watched the girl from across the street as she left the store. A block away she began hitchhiking and that was when the suspect picked her up.

Once the suspect knew that the police were using a lie to get him to confess, he had no reason to do so.

To my way of thinking, the definition of a sex offender is someone who exhibits the above five traits when interviewed. This definition isn't shared by everyone. Keep in mind that everything I'm talking about is designed to increase your interviewing skills. I'm not interested in psychologically correct terminology. With that in mind, there is another odd trait about people that meet my definition of a sex offender.

Often, sex offenders will exhibit the five traits when it would behoove them to simply tell the truth. The most vivid example of this is former President Bill Clinton and his intern, Monica Lewinsky.

To paraphrase the story, it was leaked to the media that President Clinton was having an "affair" with a female adult who was an intern at the White House. President Clinton vehemently denied any sort of sexual relationship with Lewinsky, but the allegations persisted. The president went on national television, shook his finger at the camera and repeatedly stated that he did not have a sexual relationship with Ms. Lewinsky. That was the story he stuck to until his DNA showed up on her blue dress. At that point, Mr. Clinton decided to change his story and actually talk about the "event" under investigation. In the weeks that followed, his story about what had taken place came out as follows:

1) Diminishing the severity. President Clinton re-defined the word, "sex," for all Americans. He stated that since he did not have penile-vaginal intercourse for the purpose of reproduction, he didn't really have a "sexual relationship" with her. He did imply that there other types of personal touching that took place, including oral sex and the use of a cigar. However, since his activities with Ms. Lewinsky did not involve sexual intercourse, it really wasn't that bad.

2) Blame the victim to some degree. I hate to describe Ms. Lewinsky as a victim, but in this context, she fits the criteria. Basically, Mr. Clinton stated that she kept coming to his office and what was he to do? I guess the Secret Service, FBI, Army, Navy, Air Force and Marines couldn't keep her out.

3) Attempt to control the interview. To my knowledge, Mr. Clinton has never been interviewed with regards to his relationship with Ms. Lewinsky. Instead, he asked that a list of questions be given to him in writing and then he would choose the questions he would answer. When he finally did go on camera he sidestepped most of the direct questions and reformatted the rest of them. Whenever the questioning became difficult, he had to use the restroom.

4) Never telling 100%. To my knowledge, Mr. Clinton has never described the extent of his relationship with Ms. Lewinsky. It has been referred to as an "affair," but that term implies that they were meeting at quiet, out-of-the way restaurants for candle-lit dinners and sneaking away for the week-end at some romantic getaway. As far as I know, there was never any "affair" going on between Clinton and Lewinsky. Instead, it was more like, "clear everything off the desk because she's coming over for a few minutes."

5) Never tell you something that you don't already know. Since no one had an opportunity to actually force President Clinton to speak about his relationship with Monica Lewinsky, they also did not have an opportunity to ask him about any other interns with whom he might have been involved. Also, he never clarified if he had exposed himself to Paula Jones, who was suing him during the same time frame that the Lewinsky affair came to light. President Clinton also did not speak about his relationship with a former beauty pageant winner. Therefore, by my definition, Mr. Clinton fits the behavioral profile of a sex offender.

Contrast Mr. Clinton's reaction to his relationship with Ms. Lewinsky to that of the Reverend Jesse Jackson when it was disclosed that he not only had an extra-marital affair, but had fathered a child by another woman. When this information came to light, the Reverend Jackson stated, "Yes, I did have the affair and that is my child." He went on to state that he was no longer seeing this woman and that he is paying support money for the child. He concluded by basically saying that it's nobody's damned business other than his, his wife's, the mother of the child and the child. In my opinion, he was absolutely correct. It was nobody's business except his and his immediate families. What happened publicly were some news articles for a few days about the illicit affair, and then within about a week and a half, the whole thing blew over and Rev. Jackson was back conducting his life as usual.

Had President Clinton done the same, simply come forward and said, "Yes, I am having an affair with Monica Lewinsky, so what? If the Kennedy's can do it, why can't I?" the whole thing would have blown over in about a week and nobody would have really cared about it. However, since Mr. Clinton meets my behavioral definition of a sex offender, he had to follow the five traits sex offenders always exhibit during an interview.

The techniques I'm talking about will not trick someone into confessing to something they did not do. It's more like fishing. You have to use the right bait. The above interview style is sex offender bait. A non-sex offender will not bite on it.

Keep in mind that sex offenders have all the personality traits of other humans. They can be passive, aggressive, introverted, extroverted, competitive, lazy, polite, abrasive, astute or diplomatic. They still work, pay taxes, raise families and all the rest. Being a sex offender is more like a speed bump in their personality. They may not be sophisticated criminals or even good liars. This may account for a sex offender coming down to the station to talk when common sense would tell him to run. Whether he comes to the station out of a sense of public duty or the challenge of winning the interview, once you have him in your sights, use the five trademarks to get your cop-out. He'll never see it coming.

Chapter 10

ANTI-LOGIC

Many times when investigating sex crimes, you will see what I call "anti-logic." This is some aspect of the assault that does not make any sense. Defense lawyers like to point out these illogical aspects of the assault in an attempt to influence the jury so they will feel that there is something "wrong" with the case. Quite the opposite is actually the truth.

Since rape, child molestation and other sex offenses are illogical by nature, you cannot expect the crimes to act themselves out logically. Therefore, it makes sense that illogical elements will exist within the sexual assault.

Anti-logic can actually be seen in two different ways, the first being "need-driven" behavior versus a "thought-driven" behavior. Due to the compulsive nature of some sex offenses, the "need" to commit the sex offense overpowers any "thought" to delay the behavior and/or wait until a more opportune time to attack. This often acts itself out in child molest scenarios. Frequently during family gatherings, a trusted member of the family will take a small child into an adjoining room and actually molest the child behind an unlocked door with many people nearby who could enter the room at any moment. Logic would dictate that someone should not do something this risky when the probability of being caught is so high. However, the necessity or need to commit this sex offense overpowers the logical thought processes that would prevent the behavior. This same sort of a need-driven behavior can also be seen when a suspect decides to expose himself in front of a female in a public park when there are several hundred people nearby to also see the behavior and capture him. This also happens in public libraries where the offender focuses on one potential victim and does not realize there are dozens of other people watching his behavior who might call the police.

The other aspect of anti-logic is seen when an unanticipated event or obstacle gets in the way of the sexual assault. Sex offenders often fantasize about how they are going to carry out a sexual assault and have, in essence, rehearsed it many, many times in their minds. This accounts for the skill level of even the first time sex offender. Even though he may not have acted out on the fantasy before, he has rehearsed it so many times in his mind that one might assume, sometimes mistakenly, that he has committed many similar offenses in the past. A prime example of this is the burglar-rapist who has pre-planned his sexual assault in such detail that he brings everything he will need for the assault in his "rape kit." He will disable the outside motion detectors, enter the home, prepare an exit, then contact and capture the victim, act out the fantasy, then flee.

If, during this scenario, some unanticipated event or obstacle gets in the way of the assault, he may act illogically in trying to deal with the unexpected obstacle. For example, the suspect is committing the burglary-rape and has taken many precautions to conceal his identity, but when he walks into the victim's bedroom, he sees that she has fallen asleep with the television on. The television is producing enough light to where the victim could actually see him. Even though he is wearing a nylon mask over his head that completely distorts his features, this unanticipated event is something he now has to deal with. So, instead of simply turning the television set off, or just ignoring it, he finds the comforter that has fallen from the bed and simply covers the television with it. He then puts the plan back into motion and assaults the victim per the rehearsals.

Another example of this unanticipated obstacle would be a suspect who breaks into a woman's home, anticipating she is going to be alone. However, on this particular night, she has a boyfriend sleeping with her. Logic would dictate that he should terminate the assault. But the compulsive nature of the assault forces him to continue. He adjusts his plan by kneeling down next to her, pulling back the blankets and fondling her.

The investigator has to be certain not to confuse this behavior with someone who deliberately breaks into an occupied home knowing that the boyfriend is there. This offender may want to tie up the boyfriend and rape the woman in front of him. This added power and control may have been part of the plan from the beginning.

Chapter 11

RAPE FANTASY

In order to understand sex offenders who use force to gain compliance from their victims, you have to understand the underlying rape fantasy. There are many variations of this; the most common underlying one roughly goes as follows:

The suspect feels that rape does not hurt anyone. He feels that all women want to be raped and actually need to be raped. He feels that women cannot experience true sexual pleasure because they are so concerned about the consent issue around sexual activity. Since they are fearful about consenting to sex, especially with strangers, they are so inhibited that they cannot truly have a fulfilling sexual experience. The suspect sees himself doing the woman a favor by removing the consent issue. It is his belief, that once the woman is finally free to experience a fulfilling sexual experience, she will fall madly in love with him and they will ride of into the sunset together and live happily ever after.

Psychologically, the rapist wants to make the victim feel worse than he feels about himself, which gives him not only power, but also makes him feel good.

You will see variations of this underlying theme in most of the sex offenses you investigate. Obviously, the more violent sex offenders (anger rapists, sexual sadists, etc.) do not share this fantasy with their less violent counterparts. The more angry/violent sex offenders don't care about the victims or about any such fantasy; they simply want to inflict as much pain and terror as possible.

Chapter 12

THEY DON'T GET IT

Have you ever wondered why a sex offender who knows he has committed a series of assaults in your city will come down to the police department, talk to you, give you a DNA sample that he knows will identify him to the crimes, and then go home and wait for you to come back a month later to arrest him? Well, the reason they do this is because they simply don't get it. Whatever the brain malfunction is that makes them sex offenders, also sets up a scenario where they just don't understand that they are actually going to be arrested and prosecuted. Although they logically know that what they are doing is illegal, and they logically know the steps of an investigation and the court process, there is something about them that often times prevents them from fleeing the jurisdiction and escaping incarceration. How many times have we heard the media announce that the serial rapist was living just a few blocks from his victims?

Perhaps this is another form of anti-logic. I have investigated many cases in which I identified a possible suspect, called him on the phone, asked him to come down to the station to talk. He arrives on schedule, gives me a DNA sample and confesses, all with no apparent concern about the outcome of his actions.

Perhaps there is some psychological reason for this. Perhaps being a sociopath leads to a total disregard or concern for others, and even himself. The moral of the story is: "Do not automatically eliminate a person as a suspect because he volunteers to give you DNA and seems to be very cooperative with your investigation."

I once investigated a case that is the perfect example of this. Two sisters, ages 6 and 9-years-old , where walking home from a nearby playground. They were in a hurry because they had to be home before sunset. They didn't even see the man on the sidewalk until he took the older girl by the arm. He told both girls that they "had to go with him". Twenty-five feet away some construction equipment secluded them from view and the man told the 9-year-old to stand in front of him, but not to worry because he wasn't going to hurt her. He asked the younger girl to face away.

The man unzipped his pants and while masturbating asked the nine-year-old to kneel. She asked if "it" was going to hurt and he assured her it would not and that everything would be okay, adding that he would be finished in a minute. He ejaculated onto the girl and then told both of them to hurry home.

The DNA collected from her hair did not match anyone in the data banks, but the composite drawing generated a hundred leads. Most of the tips were from women wanting me to arrest their ex-husbands for one reason or another, but one of the calls stood out from the rest. An anonymous female asked me to "check out" a man (who I'll refer to as Bob) that worked nearby and was on parole for burglary. I looked into the burglary and discovered that Bob had broken into a convent and hid in a closet so he could watch the nuns undress. Needless to say, I felt that Bob was my suspect.

On a few occasions, I've come across sex offenders that will choose victims who are non-threatening or asexual in their mind. Children, nuns, the elderly are viewed as being non-sexual by this type of offender. This means that they are all "safe" victims for him. They will not judge him and compare his "performance" to other sexual partners.

I gave Bob a call and asked him to come down to the station for a little talk. He agreed, adding that he had seen the composite that looked a lot like him, and had been wondering if the police might be calling. It took three bus transfers for Bob to get to my office. He denied the assault, but did wait for over an hour for a blood technician to arrive to draw blood for a DNA comparison. I drove him home and asked him to keep in touch.

Bob called me every two weeks for the next three months, each time asking if the DNA had come back. He even gave me his new address and phone number when he moved. When the DNA confirmed that Bob was the suspect, I called him and asked him to step outside to talk to the surveillance team that was parked in front of his residence. They gave him a ride to the station, where he was more than happy to confess. Of course, I played up the fact that he really wasn't a pedophile, he didn't hurt anyone, he had the younger girl look away, and what he was really looking for was a "hot" adult girlfriend.

Clearly, Bob didn't "get it". He had many opportunities to run away but did not. Since I ended the first interview on friendly terms, it kept him talking, right up until he went to prison. Bob had also been trying to self diagnose his behavior. He had read several books by retired FBI profiler John Douglas. Bob felt that most of the people in the books were "sick perverts" and quite different from himself.

Chapter 13

SOMETHING'S NOT RIGHT

Call it common sense, that little voice, your sixth sense, that feeling that tells you to dig a little deeper or to hold on for a second. Whatever you choose to call it, "it" has served you well on the street and you need to keep listening to "it" when working sex crimes. There are several reasons why I say this; perhaps the most important is the emotions that surround sex crimes.

Almost every city in America has a victim advocate's group, a watch dog reporter or a self proclaimed expert on child abuse, incest and rape. No one likes sex offenders so it's easy to jump on the band wagon whenever a juicy case hits the media. There are also people within your own department that will abandon logic, probable cause and the law for the emotional satisfaction of arresting a sex offender. You, the sex crimes detective, have to become the voice of reason within your agency. Don't get me wrong, I love to arrest people but I want to be certain they have actually committed a crime. The following true story will better explain my point.

One Sunday morning I got a call at home from the watch commander, wanting me to call a patrol sergeant, who was standing by for my call at a fire station in the south end of the city. The conversation went something like this:

"Sergeant, this is Howell, what's up?"

"I need you to come out here and write a search warrant, we're in the middle of a rape investigation and we need your help."

"What happened?"

"We've got one upset-crying her eyes out little girl here; looks like she was raped about half an hour ago."

"Tell me what happened."

"Our nineteen year old victim met this guy on the internet a couple of weeks ago. They exchanged e-mails and then a few phone calls. Last week

she drove to the department store where he works and they talked for a while during his break."

"How old is the suspect?"

"He's also nineteen, we've id'd him through DMV."

"So, what happened today?"

"Apparently last night the suspect called the girl and told her there was a three hour time window, when his parents would be at church, so she could come over for a while."

"And she agrees to come over?"

"Yeah, she shows up around eight thirty. They spend some time on the sofa, kissing and some touchy-feely stuff when he suggests that they go to his bedroom. She agrees, but only if he has a condom. Once in the bedroom he can't find a condom, so he promises to pull out before the rocket goes off."

"So, you're telling me that she consents to get naked with this guy?"

"Right, but once they get down to it, he don't pull out! Afterwards, she grabs her clothes and splits. She ends up at the fire station, crying her eyes out. Turns out her uncle is a fire Captain, she hoped he would be on duty, but he wasn't. So she tells the first guy she sees that she's been raped. This girl is very upset. We can't get her to stop crying."

"So what do you want me to do?"

"Well, we got a good rape here and I had a unit drive by the suspect's house and his car's gone, so I figure he split. I want to get into the house to get the sheets and blankets for bio evidence."

"But, so far I'm only seeing a breech of a verbal contract here. Don't you think we're a little short on crime elements, like force?"

"This girl is really upset, this has to be the real thing, we'll get her up to the hospital for you, while you're writing the warrant."

"But sarg,,,,"

"Hold on a second, I think one of my guys has the suspect stopped." Thirty seconds later the sergeant continues. *"Okay, we caught the suspect as he was pulling back into his driveway. Maybe you can come in and do a cold call to him."*

"How in the hell am I going to do that? Have the patrol cop hand him a cell phone!"

"Okay, we'll just arrest him for you then you can come in for the interview, while we lock down the house."

"Hold on a minute. What are you going to arrest this guy for?"

"Rape. You gotta see how hysterical this girl is."

"Why don't you just ask the guy what happened and he'll probably give you the bed sheets, then just write it all up and I'll take care of it next week."

"I know you detectives don't like us arresting people, but I think we have more than enough to hook him up."

"Okay, lets look at it this way, if this suspect was your son, would you want him arrested based on these circ's?"

"Ah,,, let me get back to you."

A couple of days later an "Information Only" report showed up on my desk in which the "suspect" stated he had consenting sex with the girl, but she became upset when he ejaculated inside of her. She was dressed and out the door before he knew it, so he dressed and drove around looking for her.

As a detective you move out of the world of *probable cause* and into the world of *beyond a reasonable doubt.* You also have to train yourself to be the forensic interviewer, the guy who is always a *neutral and non bias collector of information.* In sex crime investigations you will be interviewing a lot of people that are actually innocent, **that's okay.** Establishing innocence is just as important as establishing guilt. Don't be pushed into making an arrest based on emotions. The pressure to make a quick arrest can come from many arenas. The news media is perhaps the biggest but also the District Attorney's Office, the Chief of Police, the local rape crisis center, relatives of the victim and even your own mother may think that they know more about the case than you do. However, they don't understand the six phases of a sexual assault, the five trademarks of a suspect interview, nor do they grasp the behavioral differences between the various types of offenders.

I'm sure we all remember when NBA star Kobe Bryant was arrested in Colorado for raping a hotel employee who gone to his room after showing him around the hotel. A couple of days later the District Attorney announced the filing of criminal charges. Over the next several months the case fell apart and was ultimately dropped. In a final statement to the press Kobe Bryant said he was sorry for misinterpreting the events of that night. He believed that the young woman had consented to have sex with him, when in her mind she had not.

I have no "inside information" about this case, but I have to wonder if that isn't exactly what happened. Is it possible that to the woman a lack of saying "yes" meant "no" and to Kobe Bryant a lack of saying "no" meant "yes"? Either way, stay neutral, look at the facts and add what you know about sex offenders into your decision making.

Well, It Could Be...

This is another quagmire the sex crimes detective has to stay out of. When those around you start to explain away victim or suspect behavior with phrases like, *well it could be that the victim is changing her story because,,,,* or *well could it be that the reason the suspect raped an old woman one time and then fondled his young niece the next is because he has a split personality?* You have to be careful. Don't allow yourself to be pulled into a debate about sexually motivated behavior with those who will use rumor, half truths and urban legends to support their position. By now you know enough about sex offenders to keep it simple. They offend because it *makes them feel good.* All the varieties of offenders have this in common. Your job is to catch them, not cure them. To do so will require you to expand your thinking beyond what you were raised to think of as normal sexual activity.

A classic example is a case study frequently referred to by FBI agent Bob Morneau, who described it in my police academy and again years later during a seminar on sexually motivated offenders. Agent Morneau talked about Sergeant Pickle, who worked in a small town in central California during the 1950's and 1960's and had investigated some "strange" cases, the following being perhaps the strangest.

Living is this quite little town in a modest house was a married couple who I will call Bill and Mary. They lived there for many years, Bill walked to work each day, down Main Street to the local hardware store while Mary stayed at home. One day as Bill walked to work he suffered a massive heart attack and fell to the sidewalk. Everyone was surprised because he was only forty years old. They were more surprised when the emergency room doctor cut off his clothes and discovered that Bill was a woman.

SOMETHING'S NOT RIGHT CHAPTER 13

How could this be? Sergeant Pickle went in search of an answer.

Mary was adamant that she never knew that Bill was a woman. They had been married for 15 years and she had never seen him naked. Bill always changed clothes in the bathroom with the door locked, telling Mary that a childhood injury left his penis deformed. His embarrassment was so great that when making love Bill had insisted that she never touch his penis. They did have intercourse on a regular basis and poor Mary was at a loss to explain how she had been duped for so many years. A search of the home discovered a crudely fashioned strap-on penis, made of wood and an old jock strap.

Well, could it be that Mary was unaware of Bill's true gender? It's possible. I've interviewed women who claim to have never seen themselves naked and shower in a bathing suit to prevent any shameful nudity. I've also interviewed porn stars who let everyone see them naked. My up bringing as a Southern Baptist falls somewhere between these two extremes.

Agent Morneau hailed this story as an excellent example of how wide the definition of normal can be. After all, who knows if your neighbors are swinging-wife swappers or completely refrain from sex.

Perhaps there is a simpler answer. Is it possible that Bill and Mary were lesbians? Unable to live openly in 50's-60's small town America could they have decided to become husband and wife? Was the idea of a lesbian couple living in America's heartland so foreign that no one even considered it? The answer isn't important. There was no crime and no one to arrest, but the story broadened my thinking about what was "normal".

Many years ago I helped the FBI serve a search warrant on a home in my city, hoping to find several dismembered bodies. The FBI had an informant working inside of a photo lab that promised complete secrecy and confidential photo development. Lots of child porn was being sent to that lab by molesters from around the country, none of them knowing that an extra copy was being made for the FBI. When the informant developed several rolls of film of male genitals being cut open, weights tangling from scrotums and a penis that seemed to be mounted like a world record trout above the fire place, the FBI sprang into action. We actually had an unsolved murder/body dump that had gone cold a decade earlier, in which the genitals had been cut off the body before it was dumped a few blocks from our target house.

What we found was a small group of men and one woman who were "in to" pain and pleasure. The ultimate "high" for them was being strapped down to a wooden table and watching as their friends sliced open their scrotum with a razor blade, pulled out the testicle and started taking pictures; all without any medical training or anesthesia. To them this was normal, consenting adult sexual behavior. The leader of the group explained to me that having your friends cut open your testicles was "like having your back scratched, you know how it kind of hurts and feels good at the same time."

Shortly after the scrotum cutters I got a call from one of our local lawyers. She wanted to know if her boyfriend was normal. She went on to explain that she spends Friday and Saturday nights at his house and they have "regular sex". In the morning he will not allow her to get out of bed until she urinated on him. She wanted to know if this was "normal". I couldn't resist asking her if she was referring to his wanting to be urinated on or her actually doing it.

The moral of the story is stick to your training. Enforce the law, not emotions and use a broader understanding of sexual behavior as a guide.

Urban legends and media frenzy are a couple of other areas to be weary of. One of the largest and most famous theme parks in the world is a few miles from where I work. Every few years a story will make it to the press about a young child at the park using the restroom and while in the stall she is injected with a mystery substance that renders her unconscious. Her hair is then dyed and cut into a boy's style and her clothes are also changed. She is then smuggled out of the park. This is an interesting story, except it's not true. However, it's been around long enough that many believe it to be true and will refer to it when describing how sex offenders operate.

A couple of decades ago our country was convinced that satanic cults were operating most of our pre-schools and subjecting the youngest of children to ritualistic orgies and torture. Many adult members of these cults were "baby breeders" trying to produce as many children as possible to be sacrificed by cult leaders. The day time talk shows were interviewing former cult members who described in great detail the horrors perpetrated by hundreds of cult members. There were even support groups and therapist offering counseling to escaping members of these underground groups.

I'm not trying to debate the possible existence of such groups. Surely Charles Manson and his followers can be classified as a cult and Jim Jones orchestrating mass murder-suicide would fall into the cult category. I do have a difficult time believing that there are satanic cults on every street corner and that they have infiltrated our pre-schools.

I investigated several of these cases and unfounded each of them. I did so by keeping it simple and staying away from the *well it could be* thinking. I broke each case down to its simplest form. Interviewing each victim, witness and suspect with a cautious eye; setting aside the cult aspect of the case and just looking for sex offender behavior. I also ask simple questions like, "can two dozen cult members, an alter, three goats and a pig, fit into a $29 a night motel room?" "Is it possible for a bunch of children and adults to dance around naked in a classroom that has picture windows on three sides and a hundred people per hour walking by without noticing?"

I would suggest reading a book titled *Satan's Silence, Ritual Abuse and the Making of a Modern American Witch Hunt,* by Debbie Nathan and Michael Snedeker. This book describes how poor interviewing, politics, urban legend, failing to be a neutral-non biased interviewer and the "Well, it could be" mentality resulted in a lot of innocent people being imprisoned. As a forensic interviewer this book scared the hell out of me. As I've said before, I love arresting people and sending sex offenders to prison. I also enjoy establishing innocence and hope that I've never sent an innocent man to prison.

Chapter 14

HOW DID THEY BECOME SEX OFFENDERS?

How do people become sex offenders? Was there a one time event that forever changed their neural pathways? Was it a life time of abuse? Perhaps a genetic predisposition combined with a lack of male bonding in infancy? All of the above? I've never heard a single answer to this question nor do I have one.

I have interviewed a ton of sex offenders and the common theme is their behavior developed over time and around puberty. One of the more remarkable childhood histories was told to me by a man completely overwhelmed with the urge to suck women's toes. Two patrol cops brought him to my desk one day saying "You gotta talk to this guy."

This man (I'll call him Mark) had drawn the attention of several security guards after hours of following women around the mall. On the escalator he would stand several steps down-behind women and stare at their feet. He had been chased out of all the shoe stores and "went nuts" when a mother of three stopped for a minute, removed one shoe to rub her sore foot.

Mark was in his mid thirties and had been tossed out of almost all of the shopping centers in the county because they just didn't "understand". His eyes lighted up when I asked if he would help me to understand. To Mark it was rather simple, he had to suck women's toes and he "knew" that they wanted him to do so and he believed that women were constantly teasing him with their feet.

"How are they teasing you?" I asked.

"They know I'm watching, especially the ones wearing those pumps with the open toes. Oh My God! When they lean against the counter and the heel slips out, it drives me crazy. And they know I'm watching, they do it on purpose. They see me watching.

Mark had tried working as a shoe salesman in is younger days but never lasted more than a couple hours. The first time he helped a woman slip on a pair pumps he'd suck her toes and get fired.

Many people with severe fetishes have been in therapy for years and actually know the source of the fetish. Mark knew his and was very willing to tell me about it.

Mark was raised by his overbearing mother and two older sisters. They constantly belittled him and he could never do anything right. As punishment he was ordered to stay under his bed for a few minutes to several hours at a time. The three women would come into his room every few minutes to insure that he stayed under the bed but at least they wouldn't taunt him. Over time the only place Mark felt safe was under the bed, so he would intentionally "screw-up" so he could be punished. Somehow a combination of feeling safe, masturbating and seeing feet all blended together into a foot fetish.

Mark had been married for a short time and was able to have intercourse with his wife, but only if he was able to hold her feet at the same time. If he couldn't touch her feet he couldn't gain an erection. Mark became very agitated when asked about his fantasy, but he was more than willing to tell me. It was very specific, very well rehearsed and went something like this:

I'll be in the mall just before closing and see a woman wearing open toe shoes with just straps on the back, so I can see her heels. She won't mind that I'm watching her. We'll be the last ones to leave when the mall closes and I'll follow her out to her car. It's parked far away from anyone else and I'll follow right behind her, but she doesn't see me. When she gets in, I rush up and point a gun at her, not a real gun, just a starter pistol. She seems afraid at first but then calms down. I get into the passengers side, she knows what to do. She puts her right leg across my lap and tells me to take her shoe off. Then, you know, she lets me **suck her toes!**

Afterwards she tells me that no one has ever done that to her before and it felt really good. Then she asks if I'll go home with her and suck her toes all night long.

Mark became aroused while telling me his fantasy. I made him keep his hands on top of the table while he talked; not wanting him to masturbate in the interview room. It was scary to see how intense the fantasy was. Interviewing a toe sucker with a rape fantasy was a unique experience.

Is it possible that some men learn to eroticize violence much in the same way as Mark learned to eroticize toes? Can masturbating to thoughts of violence, fear or inflicting pain be such a strong reinforcement to the fantasy that it forms a type of addiction?

How can one pre teen boy look at the cover of a "detective magazine" and focus on the models breast while another is attracted to the look of fear in her eyes and yet another be fascinated by the way she is bound or the knife to her throat? Is there a tipping point when curiosity about what it would be like to touch the breast, cause the fear, tie the knot or hold the knife becomes super glued into the mind? I don't know the answer but I do know that it's all fair game when interviewing sex offenders.

Is it "fair" to diminish the severity of the offense by blaming a genetic disorder? Sure it is. Is it fair to blame the victim by saying that she should have known that leaving the blinds open would have attracted an admirer? Absolutely it is.

Many sex offenders study their own behavior and have come up with a rationale for what they do. Knowing this allows us to use it against them during interview. Knowing this also raises your interviewing skills from beginner to advanced and will increase your number of confessions.

Chapter 15

PUTTING IT ALL TOGETHER

The following scenarios are designed to put all of this information to the test and show how it all fits together. Taken from real cases, the outline of the circumstances will be followed by some interviewing ideas and why your thinking should have changed by now.

Example #1

A 25-year-old female calls the police department at 9:30 A.M. stating she has just been raped. She states she had been in the laundry room of a large apartment complex doing her laundry when she was approached by a male adult in his early 20's. This person had a small canvas bag with him from which he produced a handgun. She describes the handgun as being a semi-automatic with a very long barrel. The suspect tells her to turn away from him, facing a wall and undress. The victim immediately disrobes and is now standing completely naked in the laundry room with the suspect. Within 30 seconds, the suspect tells her to re-dress, which she does, and he then takes her out of the laundry room, up one flight of stairs to an elevator. Together they take the elevator to the top floor of the building, exit and take another stairwell up to a small landing area that allows access to the roof.

The landing is out of view and the suspect has the girl pull her top up over her breasts, but does not have her remove the rest of her clothes. He orders her to get on all fours and he pulls her sweat pants down to her knees. While doing so he asks if she has a boyfriend, how often they have sex and when was the last time they had sex. He then asks if she does it "doggie style". She answers "yes" to all of these questions. During the question and answer session the suspect is undressing and tells her to reach back with her left hand, hold his penis and start to masturbate him while he continues to talk. He asks her if she is "okay" or uncomfortable being on her hands and knees. She states that her arms are getting fatigued, so he tells her to stop masturbating him, sit back on her knees and take a short break.

The suspect then asks the victim if she performs oral sex with her boyfriend and again she replies that she does. He then has the victim orally copulate him for less than a minute. While doing so, she sees that the gun is laying on the floor.

The suspect then has the victim get back on all fours and he positions himself behind her so he can engage in intercourse with her. However, he has difficulty maintaining an erection and again asks the victim to reach back, grab his penis and help him insert it into her vagina. After having intercourse with her for less than two minutes, the suspect asks the victim if she engages in anal sex with her boyfriend. The victim states that she does on occasion, but she does not like that particular type of activity. The suspect then proceeds to have anal intercourse with the victim while telling her that he will be gentle with her.

After having anal intercourse with her for approximately a minute, the suspect begins to lose his erection. He withdraws from the victim and masturbates himself until he ejaculates on her back and butt.

The suspect then tells her to remove all of her clothing and hand her clothes to him while still facing away. Next, he tells her to wait on the landing for at least ten minutes. He adds that he has a friend in the apartment building with a shotgun and if this friend sees her prior to the ten-minute waiting time, his friend will kill her and her family.

As the suspect starts to leave he apologizes to her for any inconvenience he might have caused her and he also promises to mail her $200.00. He thanks her for her cooperation and leaves.

The victim waits two or three minutes prior to leaving the landing. She takes the elevator down to the second floor, gets off and runs to her apartment. She had left her door unlocked and rushes in. She immediately tells her boyfriend of the rape and the police are called.

The responding patrol officers seal off the apartment complex and find in the stairwell at the first floor level that the victim's clothing has been neatly folded and left in the corner of the stairwell.

In this scenario, the victim has clearly identified the six phases of the sexual assault: the approach, contact, capture, the sexual assault, including a whole array of statements made by the suspect, then the suspect's post-assault behaviors, followed by him leaving the scene. But, more importantly, the victim, without knowing it, has told you exactly what type of sex offender you are dealing with.

PUTTING IT ALL TOGETHER CHAPTER 15

About 40% of sex crimes occur during daylight hours, so this is not unique. His knowledge of the apartment building allows you to assume that he lives nearby. He also has to be comfortable enough with the area to loiter near the laundry room without looking out of place. If someone did call the police he could justify his presence by pointing to his house, or that of family or friends.

More important, he has brought with him a "rape kit." The canvas bag with the gun and possible other items, shows a great deal of rehearsing or pre-planning of this particular sexual assault. The gun he chose, the semi-automatic with the long barrel, is also of interest. Odds are it's a BB gun. Replicas are easier to obtain than real guns and behaviorally the suspect has deliberately set up a scenario in which he cannot hurt the victim, even accidentally. Is he using just enough force to capture her? I think so.

Did the suspect anticipate some level of resistance from the victim during the contact phase? I think so. Her quickly acquiescing to the sight of the gun was unanticipated by him. You can assume that he anticipated some degree of resistance or verbal objection by the victim prior to her following his commands. This, in essence, throws him out of rhythm. She has not followed the script that he has rehearsed in his mind. Remember that he is in a heightened state of anxiety during the contact phase. Therefore, he jumps ahead of the plan and has her disrobe in the laundry room. Once she has done this, he realizes that he is in an area where he can readily be seen and caught. He now has to get back to the plan so he has her redress. Then he forces her upstairs to where the rape is supposed to take place. This response to the unanticipated actions of the victim equals anti-logic and makes perfect sense within the context of the rape.

Once on the landing, he starts to ask her questions that are both instructional and inquisitive. He instructs her to assume a particular position on the landing for the assault to take place, while at the same time, he asks her about her sexual repertoire, and then keeps his sexual activity with her within what she normally does as a part of her consensual sex life. In essence, he is asking for permission to commit those sexual acts. Staying within the victim's normal sexual activity is his way of not hurting her. He also goes to some length to assure that she is comfortable. Remember, in his mind, he is doing the victim a favor by removing the consent element to the sexual activity, therefore, freeing her to have a truly wonderful sexual experience with him. In his mind, this is a form of consent and, therefore, he does not want to harm her.

There may be many reasons for the suspect being unable to gain or maintain an erection. In this scenario, I would entertain the possibility that the suspect has fantasized the rape activity perhaps 100 times or more, each time masturbating to ejaculation while doing so. This almost Pavlovian response to the rape fantasy has conditioned him to be able to maintain an erection and ejaculate based on a very specific scenario. The problem with this is the victim doesn't know her role and doesn't perform exactly as the suspect would like. Therefore, the suspect reverts to the "sure thing" by masturbating himself while looking at the victim, relaying on the fantasy that has always been successful for him in the past.

Once the assault is completed, he reverts back to his plan. He needs time to escape so he takes her clothes with him. He also threatens her with a fictitious armed partner. Since the suspect sees himself as a "nice guy," he leaves her clothing at the bottom of the stairwell, assuming that she is going to take the stairs all of the way to the first floor. He doesn't want her to run around naked. However, he did not anticipate that she might take the elevator and/or live on a different floor than the one on which he left the clothing.

He also apologizes to her and thanks her for her assistance in the rape. His offering to send her $200.00 on a future date is another way of easing his mind for having assaulted her. It is his way of "making up for" any inconvenience or pain he may have caused the victim.

A few weeks later, two patrol officers are contacted by a teenage couple who want to tell them about an unusual conversation they had with a friend of theirs. This friend (the suspect) told the couple that a few weeks ago; he had gone into the laundry room of a large apartment complex with a BB gun with the intent of robbing someone. He saw an attractive female in the laundry room and when she saw the gun, she immediately took all of her clothes off and stood naked in front of him. She then offered him the few dollars she had with her in exchange for leaving the complex without telling anyone about what had taken place. The suspect told his friends that he then took the money from this woman and left the apartment complex.

This statement is of great interest in that it pinpoints the location and time of the rape by these independent witnesses. More importantly, the statement shows that the suspect is doing the five things that suspects always do when they talk about the assault itself. In this case, he is diminishing the severity of it by saying it was only a robbery, and not a rape. Number two, he is blaming the victim, saying that she is the one who took her clothes off and then volunteered the money to him.

When we ultimately identified the suspect, he is a 19-year-old whose father lives three blocks away from the apartment complex. The suspect lives in a drug rehab facility, where he has been for the last two months. He has no arrest history for any sex crimes. His mother would later reveal that he was "sent away" to live with his grandparents when he was 12-years-old after playing "naked games" with his 6-year-old niece.

When contacted, the suspect volunteers to come down to the police department to talk about something that "happened" at an apartment complex near where his father lives. During the interview, he's quick to state that he was at the apartment building, with a friend. He adds that they were in the parking garage, shooting tin cans with a BB gun. He denies any knowledge of the rape. Ultimately, he talks about having bumped into an old girlfriend, going to the upstairs landing, and having sex with her. However, he has difficulty remembering her name, phone number, and how they first met.

Since I know that different types of sex offenders don't like each other, and since this particular suspect is clearly a power rapist, it is easy to use this information against him to get a confession. The line of questioning went something like this:

> *"I've been doing this for a long time. Actually, I retired last month and was called back to work this case. And I know that there are different profiles for people that commit sex offenses. There's even one for girls that make up stories about being raped. From what this girl is telling us, I know she's not making it up. In fact, I know that the guy who assaulted her is an approval seeking power rapist.*
>
> *I don't think you ever would have hurt this girl. I think you went there with the hopes of finding a girl who would engage in consensual sex with you and perhaps become your girlfriend. I think you deliberately used a BB gun instead of a real gun so you could not hurt her. I think the girl freaked out when she saw the gun and undressed. So you went ahead and acted out the fantasy about having sex with her. Had she resisted in the slightest way, you would have disengaged your assault and left without hurting her. From what the girl told us, we know you are not a "serial killer," and we also know she is not someone who is making up a false report. I feel real comfortable that you fall in that category of a type of sexual offender who would never hurt a potential victim, but is hoping for a victim who would easily comply."*

CHAPTER 15   PUTTING IT ALL TOGETHER

In this particular case, the suspect immediately responded by stating, "Yes, you're right; I raped her." He then talked at length about the planning of the crime and how he had been waiting outside of the laundry room for two hours. He added that several women had entered the laundry room, but they looked a little "scary", so he didn't approach them. He did admit to having intercourse with the victim, but denied the oral and anal sex. He confirmed promising to send her $200 and thanking her for her cooperation.

I let him "win" several times during the interview. The suspect went on to detail that he had been fantasizing about raping a woman for the last couple of years, and in his canvas bag, he had not only the BB gun, but condoms, Saran Wrap, latex gloves and a surgical mask. On the morning of the assault he had shaved all of his pubic hair and was planning to mummify himself with the Saran Wrap, to prevent leaving any DNA at the scene. Unfortunately for him the assault happened faster than he had imagined and he forgot to follow his own plan.

Example #2

A 19-year-old female states that while working at the local supermarket, she was instructed to go out at night and collect the shopping carts left in the parking area. When she went to the side of the building which is not very well lit, she was grabbed from behind by two unidentified assailants and hit in the head with an unknown object and lost consciousness. She did not awaken until two hours later when her husband was attempting to pick her up and put her into their car. At this time, her pants were pulled down past her butt, and her blouse and bra had been removed. She can only assume that she was sexually assaulted, or at least that someone had attempted to rape her, and added that someone stole her wedding ring off her finger, which had been given to her by her grandmother.

The husband states that he had gone to the supermarket to pick his wife up after work, however, she was not inside the store and no one in the store could recall seeing her for several hours. He decided to look for her in the darkened back and side lots of the store instead of going across the parking lot to the open pizza parlor. He decided to do this because in the last two months, his wife has been attacked on three other occasions. Each time, the suspects were unrelated to each other, unidentified, and each one of them stopped short of having actually raped her.

A quick conversation with the store manager reveals that the victim is a very poor employee and they were thinking about terminating her within the next few days. Also, when he asked her to go out into the parking lot to retrieve the shopping carts, she was fearful to do so, wanting to take a razor blade box cutter with her in case someone tried to attack her. She was fearful to go outside alone and alluded to some prior "attacks." Investigation of the scene reveals that the stores box cutter had been used to cut off the victim's shirt sleeves, which in turn were used to bind her hands in front of her.

Obviously, this case is full of red flags. The first being the probability of this woman having been sexually assaulted three separate times, by three separate suspects, within two months. Also, if the victim had been laying unconscious for two hours, what are the odds of someone finding her before her husband? The victim did have a small abrasion on her forehead at the hairline, and is taken to the hospital for treatment.

At the hospital, the ER doctor informs you that the bump on her head is superficial and would not have caused her to lose consciousness. He adds that had she been unconscious for two hours, she would have had a concussion, which would still be affecting her at this time. However, since she is talking clearly and has no obvious indications of any sort of a brain injury, it can be concluded that the forehead injury was self-inflicted. In this scenario, however, since the victim is alleging that she was knocked unconscious immediately, you are unable to derive from her the six phases of the sexual assault, and/or any dialogue between her and the suspects.

Therefore, you need to focus in on the missing wedding ring. Due to its sentimental value, she probably did not throw it away or sell it. So, you head to the supermarket, this time looking for the women's lounge. Along the wall are some cheap lockers used by the employees to store their belongings while they work. Inside the victim's locker, you find her purse; inside the purse, you find her wallet; inside the secret compartment inside the wallet, you find the "missing" wedding ring. It doesn't take a rocket scientist to realize that two suspects did not hit this woman over the head, partially disrobe her, take off her wedding ring and place it back into her wallet in her locked locker. The only conclusion you can draw from this is that the victim has a history of falsely reporting sex crimes in order to divert attention away from other actions in her life, this particular one being her pending termination from this job. Some of the other sexual assaults involved an excuse for her to be failing classes in school and for loss of other jobs.

Example #3

You receive a report of several third grade girls having been touched inappropriately by their teacher during class. Eight of the girls in the classroom come forward and state that during the morning and afternoon reading exercises, they are called up to the teacher's desk and asked a question about the assignment. During this time, the teacher would place his hand on the small of their backs and run his fingers down past the belt line of their clothing, to an area at the top of their butts. The girls add that he would do this briefly then remove his hand, and that he had been doing so for much of the school year. This happened so often that all the kids in the class had witnessed it.

One girl reported that twice while sitting next to the teacher, he placed his hand on her thigh and through the pants opening of her shorts, touched the elastic part of her underwear in her vaginal area.

All of the girls identify yet another girl in the class who appears to be the teacher's favorite student. This is because she spends all of her school recess and lunch time in the class room with the door locked, alone with her teacher.

The girls go on to state that during lunch today, they all went to the girls' restroom where they discussed what was happening. They were trying to determine if they had been molested since their parents had always told them that a "child molester" would be a stranger who would kidnap them. Since the teacher was not a stranger, and since the touching was relatively minor, they were having difficulty determining if this was something they should tell anyone about. Ultimately, one of the girls decided to tell the school nurse, which started the investigation.

When the suspect/teacher is contacted, he denies any inappropriate nature to his touching. He states that he is simply a "very touchy type of person" and that the girls must have misinterpreted his actions. He also theorized that the girls had entered into a conspiracy to get him into trouble for some unknown reason.

The interesting aspect of what the girls are really saying is a description of the pipeline theory of victim selection and anti-logic (Fig 14) next page). Since the suspect has a large pool of potential victims to draw from, he goes through a selection process to ascertain which child is more susceptible to being molested to a greater degree. He touches the girls somewhat innocently and, if they pull away, he stops. If they don't pull away, he proceeds to see how far he can go. Ultimately, he finds a child who is very susceptible to being molested, normally due to a lack of a strong family structure, and molests that girl to a greater extent.

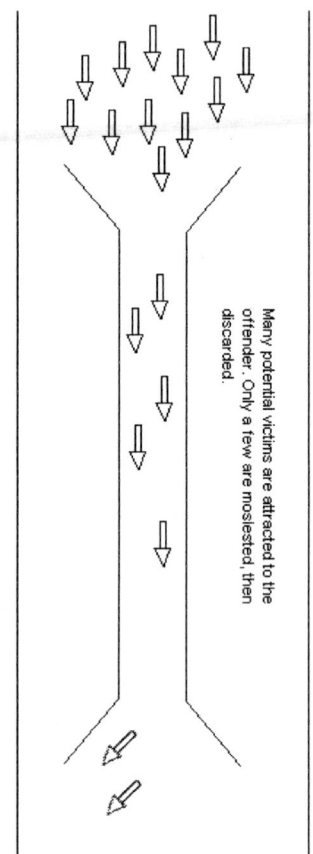

(Fig. 15) FBI Pipeline Theory

The girls also identify anti-logic, in that it is not a logical behavior for an educated man to be molesting school girls in broad daylight in front of an entire classroom. However, this is perfectly normal within the context of a sex offender, who is acting out of a need driven behavior as opposed to a thought-driven behavior which would cause him to delay the molest, or do it more clandestinely.

Since the girls talk about the touching having taken place over several months, it is logical to assume that there are other victims in previous classes this man has taught. An extensive investigation does reveal other victims dating back several years that have been touched in a similar fashion. The difficulty in prosecuting such a case is that most of the girls describe touching that is marginally illegal. The one girl still in the pipeline isn't likely to talk, and her parents will probably block your attempts to interview her, stating that if there was a problem, "they would handle it."

The case is further hampered by the suspect's lawyer halting any further interviews. Many of the parents will also impede the investigation by siding with the teacher. They don't want to believe that their kids have been molested, so it's easier to turn a blind eye. Even explaining the pipeline theory to them is a waste of time. Your best bet is to look for a former victim of more overt touching. This child will no longer be in the pipeline and may be willing to talk. Remember that the offender wants to make himself feel good. This simple touching satisfies that need. Intercourse and oral sex may not be in the equation for him.

As a side note, the girls getting together to talk about the molestation is an age-appropriate coping mechanism for kids this age. Defense lawyers love to point to this as evidence of a conspiracy by evil 8-year-olds.

Example #4

You respond to a local grammar school due to a suspected child molest report being made by the school nurse. Upon arrival, you find that the victim, a fifth grade girl, has told her best friend "in confidence" about sexual touching going on between her and her mother's live-in boyfriend. The victim's friend then tells the school nurse; the school nurse, in turn, calls the police.

You have the victim girl brought into the office where you can speak privately with her. She tells you that her biological mother and father are divorced and she lives with her mother and the mother's live-in boyfriend. She states that for the last year, whenever the mother is out of the house, the boyfriend puts on his favorite black dress, along with a woman's wig.

He adds eyeliner and lipstick and then asks her to join him in the bathroom once he is totally "dressed." He produces a rubber dildo and helps her insert it into his rectum. Her role is to move this dildo in and out of his rectum while he masturbates and watches himself in the bathroom mirrors. The child is never asked to disrobe; she is never touched by him and, after each one of these events, he gives her two-dollars and orders her to keep his secret.

The victim telling an age mate about the molestation is very common. If all the adults in your life have failed you, a friend is the only one to turn to. Just like the girls in the earlier example, this is an age-appropriate coping mechanism for children in this type of situation.

The victim is describing approach, contact, capture, the sexual assault itself, and the post-assault behaviors. She is describing a level of force that is nothing more than the parental figure inside the home telling her to do something with no real threat or violence against her. For her to be able to fabricate a story like this would require information about sexual behaviors that are far beyond her realm of experience. She is describing someone with multiple paraphilic behaviors. The mother's boyfriend obviously likes to cross-dress in addition to being both an exhibitionist and a voyeur, in that he both exposes himself and watches himself in the mirrors at the same time. The girl simply helps facilitate the multiple behaviors by helping him with the dildo. After the activity is complete, the post-assault behavior is for the suspect to give the child some money and tell her not to tell anyone.

In doing background work on the family, you find that the suspect is actually married to the child's mother. The reason for the "living together" charade is that the mother and the suspect are actually first cousins. You also discover that the child's uncle, on her mother's side of the family, is currently serving multiple life terms in prison for a series of burglary-rapes.

The best way to approach the suspect during an interview is to tell him you understand that real sex offenders are like his cousin/brother-in-law (the one who is in prison) and that he (the suspect) would never actually hurt a child. You tell him you understand that some people have multiple sexual behaviors they like to engage in and that sometimes, when the wife will not cooperate in assisting in these behaviors, they seek out the aid of someone else to help them. In this case that someone was just too young. You tell him that he really is not a "child molester" or even a "rapist," but simply acted inappropriately by using the child to assist him in acting out

CHAPTER 15   PUTTING IT ALL TOGETHER

his sexual fantasies. This "understanding" of the suspect's predicament is your best method for soliciting admissions or a confession from him.

Example #5

Two high school aged sisters, ages 13 and 15, report that they were late to school one morning. Not wanting to come on campus during the middle of class, they decided to wait until the morning recess before walking onto campus. They waited across the street in the small food court. It was only fifteen minutes until the next recess. They are approached by a male adult who showed them a police badge and tells them that he is a truant officer. He asks them to accompany him to his office so he can contact their parents, the school and make inquiries as to why they are not in class.

The girls accompany the suspect to an area behind the food court and into an abandoned building, strewn with old furniture and home to several transients. Once there, he orders both girls to disrobe. He tells them that he has a gun and if they do not comply, he will use it. They never see a gun. Both girls disrobe and are told to turn around. Next, he has them lean over the back of a filthy sofa. He then rapes both of the girls from behind, starting with the 13-year-old. During the course of the rape, he asks the girls about their sexual histories. The 13-year-old indicates that she has never had sex before; the 15-year-old states that she has had sex on two prior occasions. The suspect tells the 13-year-old that she obviously needs to "catch up" with her sister and he proceeds to rape her for a longer length of time than the older girl.

While having sex with the 13-year-old, he tells her that she needs to move her hips back and forth to make it more pleasurable for her. After the suspect ejaculates, he tells both girls to count to 100 before they re-dress and leave the building. He then flees.

The girls count to 50 before dressing and running to school. They ask the principal to call the police.

In this scenario, the girls clearly identify the six phases of the sexual assault: the approach being his walking up to them as they are eating; contact being his identifying himself as a truant officer; capture being the isolation of the girls in the abandoned room and stating that he has a gun; the sexual assault itself, during which his conversation is both instructional and inquisitive. The post-assault behaviors involve his telling the girls to count to 100 before re-dressing, then fleeing on foot.

DNA linked this particular suspect to ten other rapes in the county. However, the M.O. of the other rapes was completely different. In one of the prior cases, he broke into a home around 9:00 A.M., waited until noontime when the woman came home for lunch. He captured her at knife-point in the living room and raped her on the floor. In another case, a group of teenagers were walking on an isolated road late one night when he pulls up beside them in his car. He points a gun at the group and asks the group to pick one of the girls to accompany him. One of the girls was chosen; she gets into the car with him; he drives her about two miles away and rapes her in the front seat of the car. Yet another of the rapes involves a girl walking home in the evening hours near a freeway overpass. The suspect ran up behind her, grabbed her from behind, took her into the bushes adjacent to the on-ramp, where he raped her from behind and took one of her shoes. In yet another rape, the suspect watched two girls surfing in front of their beach house one morning. Later they were driven to school by their mother. The suspect broke into the home, presumably to wait for the two girls to return. However, the mother returns home first and after making inquiries as to when the girls would return, the suspect rapes the mother. However, he has difficulty maintaining an erection and has to masturbate in order to reach ejaculation. He takes the mother's cellular telephone as he leaves. When he calls a few minutes later, he threatens her not to call the police because he is watching her.

From the last rape, a lead was developed from a parking citation. As it turns out, the day of that rape was street-sweeping day and the suspect had parked his car on a street that should have been clear for street-sweeping. The parking ticket led to a male in his 40's who lived in a neighboring county and who had no arrest record. DNA links all of the cases together and the suspect refuses to give a DNA sample. After several attempts to interview him, he finally "lawyers up."

The next avenue of investigation is to contact his wife. She talks about what a loving husband he is and what a great father he is to their three children. She states it would be impossible for him to ever rape anybody because he is always home by 5:30 PM. He has dinner with his family and spends the entire night at home until he goes to work in the morning. However, her statement contradicts that of the neighbors, who state that he is always leaving in the evening hours and returning after midnight. They add that his work schedule is very sporadic, and he has been chronically unemployed for the last year. The neighbors have heard heated arguments between the couple. His driving history shows a 2 AM speeding ticket.

In this scenario, the wife is playing the role of the "enabler," in that she is trying to balance the scale within her family of good and bad.

Basically, her husband is being the bad person in the family, but she wants to portray a good home environment. Therefore, she portrays him as being overly good, therefore balancing the scales. It is much like the non-drinking spouse in an alcoholic family. The non-drinking spouse tries to overcompensate for the drinking and bad behaviors of the alcoholic spouse.

This type of suspect is probably going to be too arrogant to submit to a detailed interview. He sees law enforcement and anyone from the government as being beneath him. Ultimately, his DNA is obtained via search warrant, and he is linked to the crimes.

Because of his arrogant and narcissistic demeanor, you can predict that he will never allow the case to go to trial. Instead, he would rather plead guilty to the charges and go to prison as opposed to letting people whom he sees as inferior to himself sit in judgment of him. Also, this keeps the true facts of the case from ever becoming public knowledge. This is his way of controlling his environment.

This is a clear example of the difference between M.O. and Fantasy. In sex crimes, M.O. is the process that brings the suspect into contact with the victim. As seen in this case, the M.O. varied widely. The fantasy acts itself out after capture is complete. Re-interviewing all the victims revealed an almost identical dialogue between suspect and victim between the capture and assault phases. He was very interested in victims with limited sexual partners and preformed better with the inexperienced girls and in a few cases he took a shoe. We never figured out why, nor did we ever find the shoes.

Example #6

A 30-year-old female reports that while shopping at an upscale mall, she returns to her car that is parked on the upper level of the parking structure, even though there are many parking places on the lower levels. While walking to her car, an unknown assailant pulls up beside her, grabs her from behind and throws her into the front seat of the car. She is instructed not to look at the suspect as he drives away. Even though it was broad daylight, she never got a look at him. She states that after being driven for perhaps 30 minutes, the suspect parked in an alley. She is still being instructed to keep her face turned to the side so she cannot see him. The suspect then pulls the victim's dress over her hips and pulls her pantyhose down to around her ankles in one swift motion. He spends the next two hours fondling her vagina and inserting his fingers into her vagina while calling her a "slut" and "whore" and other derogatory terms. He also threatens to kill her if she looked at him. Ultimately he rapes her, using a condom.

During the two-hour ordeal, the suspect repeatedly threatens the victim with death, stating he would kill her and dump her body in a location where it would never be found. At the end of the assault, the suspect drove her back to the parking structure where he found her. He apologized for having inconvenienced her, tells her that his girlfriend is pregnant and he hasn't had any sex in a long time, and that is why he had to do this to her. He tells her to get out of his car without looking at him, which she does, and he drives off.

The victim then calls the police and reports the rape; however, she cannot give any sort of vehicle or suspect description that might aid in the capture of the suspect. She is taken for a medical exam, which reveals the presence of two small pieces of latex inside her vagina. These are later determined to be pieces of latex from two different colored condoms.

The victim says she understands there is no way the suspect can be identified and she simply wants to put the whole incident behind her and go on with her life.

This case has some problems. The first is the lack of any suspect or vehicle description. Women who falsely report crimes often times do so with a deliberate lack of suspect information so that no innocent person will be apprehended and/or prosecuted. There is also an issue with the approach, contact, capture, etc. in this case. The victim states that when she is "captured," the suspect continues to threaten her even though she is complying with his demands. This creates an area of concern.

If the suspect was a "power rapist," which the majority of rapists are, he would only use enough force to capture her. Once he has captured her, he would fall into the sexual assault phase, the acting out of the fantasy, and there would no longer be a need for him to threaten her in order to gain compliance. Also, if he were a power rapist, he would not use derogatory terms toward her. Instead, he would engage in a conversation that was inquisitive and instructional.

If he was an anger-rapist he might continue to physically threaten her and use derogatory terms. However, he would also use an excessive amount of force in order to capture her. It's doubtful that the anger rapist would apologize to the victim afterwards, and offer an excuse for his behavior.

This particular case went unsolved for several months until the victim's best friend came forward and volunteered a different scenario. She told the police that the victim has been having an affair for several months. She meets her lover on the top level of the parking structure, leaving her car and driving to a nearby motel. On the day of the rape, the victim and boyfriend overslept putting her behind schedule. She needed to account for her time away from her family so she fabricated the rape. The colored condoms were remnants of those used by her boyfriend.

When confronted with this information, the victim admitted to making a false police report and was ultimately prosecuted for that offense.

Example #7

A female in her mid 20's reports that she and some girlfriends went out to a local dance club for a "girls' night out." While at the club, she had several mixed drinks, but never lost consciousness and was always aware of what she was doing. As the evening progressed, she saw a man sitting at the bar that she could only describe as having "big biceps." She was attracted to his physique and went over to talk with him. She recalls kissing him at the bar and, ultimately, they moved to an alcove area near the women's restroom, where they kissed and he began to fondle her breasts over her clothing.

After a few minutes, he suggested that they go out to his car to "listen to his stereo." She agreed and left the dance club with him, walking hand-in-hand to his car. She then got into the passenger side. He suggested they drive to a more remote part of the parking area, and she agreed. They drove to an isolated area of the parking lot where no other vehicles were parked nearby. The suspect suggested that the stereo speakers in the back seat were better than those in the front and they should move to the back for better listening. The victim agreed. Being naked would surely make the stereo sound better, so they both undressed.

While sitting naked in the back seat of the car they engaged in all of the behaviors former President Clinton said weren't really sex. She said she agreed to perform oral sex on the suspect; he, in turn fondled her breasts, and inserted his fingers into her vagina. He also performed oral sex on her, which was consensual in nature, during which time she had an orgasm.

She continued to kiss the suspect while masturbating him with her right hand. The victim further stated she "suddenly" realized the suspect wanted to have intercourse with her. She added that she was "frozen with fear" and did not know what to do. Somehow the suspect "jumped on top of me and spread my legs apart." She didn't know what to do or say. The suspect then inserted his penis into her vagina and had intercourse with her for several minutes. The intercourse was very painful and the only way she could relieve the pain was to wrap her legs around the hips of the suspect. Additionally she decided that if she was going to be raped, she might as well go ahead and have another orgasm, so she did.

After the "ordeal" was over, both she and the suspect were dressing. During this time, she reached into her purse and withdrew a pencil and paper. She demanded to know the name and phone number of the suspect; however, he refused. She told him, "You can't just have sex with a girl and not tell the girl who you are." His response was, "Yes, I can. I just wanted to f—— you. Besides, you're too ugly to introduce to any of my friends." The victim began to cry and the suspect ordered her out of the car. Moments later he drove off, leaving her standing in the parking lot. She walked back to the dance club where she re-joined her friends. They noticed she was crying and asked her what had happened. She stated, "I've been raped."

This is clearly a case of buyer's remorse. The victim doesn't want to believe she is the type of girl that would have sex with a complete stranger. In order to save face with her friends and herself, she has to reconstruct the event in her mind to be a rape. This type of victim will never concede that the activity was consensual. To do so would mean that she was one of those "bad girls" and her self-image would never allow for such an admission. The best way to resolve this case is to tell her that there are some issues with the force element of the crime and it is doubtful that such a case would ever be prosecuted, even if the suspect were located.

Example #8

You receive a report of an 11-year-old boy who has taken a roll of paper towels, set them on fire, and thrown them into the open bedroom window of an adult male living in his neighborhood. The paper towels set the drapes on fire, but the fire is quickly extinguished. The patrol officers responding to the fire call tell you they are surprised that someone would do such a thing to the adult because he always has an entourage of 10 to 13-year-old boys around him, and they considered him a "Pied Piper" of the neighborhood. They state that he always has this entourage of boys who are never older, never younger, and never female, with him every place he goes. You learn that he is a self-proclaimed martial arts expert and has a small studio in the garage where he lives. You also learn that he is renting a room from a single mother who has a 13-year-old son living with her.

A quick check of local records on all of the boys in the suspect's entourage reveals that most of them have had minor contacts with law enforcement and have frequently been truant from school. There also appears to be a lack of family structure in their homes.

Remembering the pipeline model for victim selection, one might think that the boy who set the suspect's house on fire had been drawn through the pipeline and has now been discarded out the other end. Being discarded, he decides to retaliate by setting the suspect's room on fire. You also have to be suspicious of why this adult has an entourage of young boys, all in a specific age range.

You also want to be suspicious of his living arrangements. Living in the home of the single Mom gives him a good cover. The appearance of a boyfriend-girlfriend relationship makes him more acceptable to the neighborhood. What might be happening is that he is using that woman's 13-year-old son as a recruiter for other potential victims. Specifically, this boy would go out and tell his friends that there is this very strong-cool guy living at his home and if they want to, they can come over and "hang out" with him and he will teach them karate. This creates a scenario where many potential victims are attracted to one end of the pipeline. Those who are most vulnerable are selected, molested over time, and discarded. Since it is likely that those kids, who are still inside the pipeline, are closely aligned to the suspect and will not "give him up," you have to focus your interview on those who have been discarded.

You start with the boy who set the apartment on fire. He ultimately discloses some sexual fondling between himself and the suspect. However, he is not going to give you very much information. You have to keep in mind that he is only likely to tell you about 25% of the sexual activity between him and the suspect, and he'll keep the other 75% to himself.

You also discover that the suspect is going by the a.k.a. of "Rambo," however, his real name reveals a lengthy criminal history But none of his priors are sex crimes. He has also been on the cover of a local martial arts magazine as a self-proclaimed expert of the martial arts. He's been using this magazine to attract boys to him as potential victims.

Your original victim is able to point you toward the other boys who have been victimized. This leads to additional interviews. Once the suspect is arrested you have a shot at some of the other kids. Some may talk about the molestation; many will not.

This type of suspect obviously has a sexual preference for boys of a specific age. You can assume that this is truly his sexual preference. Because of that, you know he will not like anyone who would actually rape young boys or who would physically hurt them. Also, he will not like offenders who molest much younger children. Knowing this, you approach the interview by saying something like:

"I need you to help me out in understanding exactly who you are. I'm afraid that the general public is going to perceive you as one of those 'child molesters' who is hanging around the school yard with a bag of candy and kidnapping children, raping them, and leaving them for dead. I don't think that's who you are. I think that perhaps something else has happened here. I can see that these boys have very uninvolved families and that perhaps you stepped in to help them in some way and somehow, that helping got out of hand, which led to some sort of inappropriate touching between you and the boys. I'm sure that your intent was to help them and not hurt them, but I need you to tell me that so I can understand who you are, so I can present that information to the court. My job as a detective is to be a neutral and non-biased collector of information. I need you to fill in the other side of the equation for me..."

Example #9

A female Asian in her late teens comes to you and states she is attending extension courses at the computer lab at the local junior college. She states that each student sits in a small cubicle while working on a computer and the teacher, a male in his mid 50's, comes around to each cubicle and assists the students on each of their projects. The girl goes on to say that on several occasions, this teacher has stood behind her while she was doing her assignments. On many occasions, he has reached his right hand down the opening of her blouse and fondled both of her breasts. Due to the configuration of the cubicles, it is possible that none of the other students actually witnessed this. She adds that after being fondled for a few seconds, she would object by simply moving her body to the side and pulling away from the suspect, at which time he removed his hand from her blouse and moved on to assist other students. This has happened approximately 10 times and she has been too embarrassed to tell anyone about this until now.

CHAPTER 15   **PUTTING IT ALL TOGETHER**

You, as a detective, arrange for a "cold telephone call" to the suspect by the victim. He readily talks about the fondling and tells the girl that he is sorry if he offended her.

When you make telephone contact with the teacher, you do not tell him about the cold call, but simply ask him about his relationship with this student. He immediately says, "Yes, I did it." He goes on to explain that for some reason, he is drawn to this particular student and that when he stands behind her, he is able to look down her blouse and see part of her breasts, and he simply can't help but reach inside her blouse and fondle her. He states he has never engaged in activity like this in the past, and he simply doesn't know what has come over him. He readily admits to all 10 counts of fondling the girl, and admits to becoming sexually aroused and gaining an erection during the time that he does it.

Conclusion

So much for my theory about sex offenders always diminishing the severity and blaming the victim to some degree. Occasionally, you will find a sex offender who readily admits to his behavior and is openly apologetic and remorseful for it. When this happens, just accept it as an early Christmas gift, go ahead and prosecute the offender then move on to your next case.

Appendix A

RAPE TRAUMA SYNDROME

Victims of rape suffer a significant degree of physical and emotional trauma during the rape, immediately following the rape and over a considerable time period after rape. The symptoms that are consistently felt over and over by rape victims are clustered into a group and classified as the rape trauma syndrome. This syndrome has two stages: the immediate or acute phase, in which the victim's lifestyle is completely disrupted by the rape crisis, and the long-term process, in which the victim must reorganize this disrupted lifestyle.

During the acute phase, the rape victim experiences both emotional and physical reactions. The primary emotional feeling expressed is the fear of physical injury, mutilation and death. These symptoms are an acute stress reaction to the threat of being killed, and it is this main feeling of fear that explains why victims develop the rape trauma syndrome.

Although the immediate emotional reactions of rape victims vary, there appears to be two general categories of emotions shown: expressed or controlled. The victim displaying the expressed style will demonstrate feelings such as anger, fear and anxiety while the person showing the controlled style masks their feelings and displays a calm, composed outward appearance. Also during the acute phase, many victims report feeling irritated with people in the first few weeks after the rape and are prone to mood swings such as depression and emotional outbursts. The victim might also experience feelings of humiliation, degradation, guilt, shame, embarrassment, self-blame, anger and revenge. The victim finds that although she tries to continually block the assault from the mind, it keeps coming back.

Besides the immediate emotional reaction during the acute phase, the person also displays physical reactions. Because rape is forced sexual violence against a person, victims describe a wide gamut of physical reactions. Some victims describe a general feeling of soreness all over their bodies, while others specify the body area of the assailant's force. Other types of physical reactions during the acute stage include sleeping and eating pattern disturbances. In terms of sleep disturbances, rape victims have considerable difficulty with disorganized sleep patterns, complaining that they cannot fall asleep or find they wake up during the night and are not able to fall back to sleep. Victims who have been attacked while sleeping in their own beds might awake each evening at that time again and find they cannot fall back to sleep. Also, it is not uncommon for victims to scream out in their sleep. Eating pattern disturbances include such complaints as a decrease in appetite, stomach pains or remarks that the food doesn't taste quite right.

The second stage of the syndrome is the long-term process during which the victim must reorganize their disrupted lifestyle. The rape represents a disruption in the lifestyle of the victim, not only during the immediate days and weeks following the incident, but well beyond that to many weeks and months.

The victim has to cope with various symptoms during the long-term reorganization process. Changes in lifestyle is one of the symptoms. The rape often upsets the victim's normal routine of living. Many victims are able to resume only a minimal level of functioning even after the acute phase ends. Some victims go to school or work but are unable to be involved in social activities, while other victims respond to the rape by staying home or venturing out only with a friend.

Also included many times in the lifestyle change is a strong desire to get away, and a common response is to turn for support to family members not normally seen on a daily basis. Changing residence specifically because of a rape is another common response during this period of time. Many victims also change their telephone number, requesting an unlisted number.

A continuing problem from the acute stage is the occurrence of dreams and nightmares. During the second phase, victims typically report two types of nightmares. The first type of dream places the victim in a similar situation as during the rape. During this dream, the victim tries to get out of the situation that led to the rape but fails. The second type of nightmare occurs as time progresses, and the dream's content is still filled with horror as the rape victim sees themselves committing acts of violence against other people. Although the power in this second type of dream may represent mastery, the victim still has to deal with this violent self-image.

Another common psychological defense of victims during the long-term process stage is the development of fears and phobias specific to the circumstances of the rape. Victims will develop phobic reactions to a wide variety of circumstances. These include the avoidance of crowds, fear of being alone, intense feelings of insecurity and disillusionment regarding the victim's safety in the world. The rape victim might also find that they might have diminished sex drive or a fear of sex. This is especially upsetting if the victim has never had any experiences before the rape. The victim might find a general loathing for their body, feeling that it is their fault that the rape took place. Fears might also be specific to the characteristics of the assailant. For example, the victim might become anxious of the odor of alcohol, gasoline or cigarettes if the rapist possessed such an odor. A female rape victim might also find that she has acquired a generalized fear of men.

There are two variations of the rape trauma syndrome. The first of the two is called the compounded reaction to rape, during which the victim experiences not only the previously noted symptoms but also a reactivation of symptoms of a previous existing condition such as a psychiatric illness. The other variation is called the silent reaction to rape during which various symptoms occur but without the victim ever mentioning that a rape had occurred.

Counseling of rape victims is based on the following assumption: That the rape represents a crisis which disrupts the victim's lifestyle in four areas—physical, emotional, social and sexual. Victim counseling is an issue-oriented crisis treatment model with the focus of the initial interview and follow-up being on the rape incident, and the goal being to help the victim return to their previous level of lifestyle as quickly as possible. The victim is viewed as needing emergency services and the rape is viewed as a crisis situation. Previous problems not associated with the rape are not considered priority issues for discussion in the counseling. Additional professional help is needed for victims with compounded reactions.

APPENDIX B

INDICATORS OF FALSE ALLEGATIONS OF SEXUAL ASSAULT BY STRANGERS

In a seminar conducted by Roy Hazelwood, of the FBI's Behavioral Studies Unit, the following characteristics were reported as having occurred in enough falsely alleged cases of sexual assault by a stranger to be significant. These circumstances do not prove false allegations. When the case is looked at in its entirety, these characteristics could indicate a false allegation.

I. **The Victim**
   A. The underlying motive for false allegation is a need for attention.
   B Look for a disruption in family life.
   C The victim suffers from low self-esteem.
   D There are interpersonal problems with someone important in their lives.
   E. Distress or positive events in recent life/stressful occurrences.
   F There may be a history of undiagnosed illness (e.g., constantly going to the doctor with ailments that are false).
   G. The victim may have made similar complaints in another area (usually of prior residence).

II. **The Allegation**
   A. The report may be delayed and/or reported to someone other than law enforcement.
   B. The victim may be indifferent to her injuries.
   C. Details may be extremely detailed or extremely vague.

D. When interviewed, the victim will attempt to steer the discussion away from areas dangerous to her. (i.e., information you need to prosecute someone, location and/or description of suspects).

E. The victim will attempt to steer you toward safe areas as the amount of force used and her resistance.

F. There may be no reluctance to have her wounds/injuries photographed by someone of the opposite sex.

G. The suspect(s) may be multiple assailants or a single assailant who is huge and overpowering.

H. The suspect may be described as a total stranger or a friend of an unrecalled friend.

I. The sexual acts will not be outside the victim's normal repertoire.

J. Defense wounds will be inconsistent with the reported angle of attack.

K. Violence reported is vigorously physically resisted.

L. Injuries may be reported with indifference.

M. More serious wounds are in areas normally covered by clothing. Less serious injuries are in areas normally exposed.

N. Wounds do not involve sensitive areas of the body. They can lead up to the sensitive area but will stop short.

O. Messages may be carved in the body. (This never has been done in a righteous sexual assault.)

P. Wounds are either horizontal or lateral on the body.

Q. Wounds are anatomically oriented (usually the breast area).

APPENDIX B INDICATORS OF FALSE ALLEGATIONS OF SEXUAL ASSAULT BY STRANGERS

III. Evidence

A. Damage to clothing is inconsistent with the report.

B. Damaged clothing is clothing that is usually not worn by the victim e.g., old clothes.

C. The victim "just now" recalls prior occurrences such as obscene phone calls or messages.

D. The scene does not support the story.

E. Notes allegedly left by the suspect are "cut and paste" or block letters that are usually threatening or sexually obscene. The note looks like something out of the movies.

F. Reported break-ins where there is theft or damage to property.

IV. Other Considerations

A. The victim may attempt to establish a relationship with the investigator.

B. The victim may claim, "You are not asking the 'right' questions."

C. There may be an abnormal dissatisfaction with the investigator.

D. There may be a continuous recall of additional facts.

E. There may be an apparent lack of interest in the investigation.

V. Recommendations

A. Don't confront the victim until you are convinced the allegation is false.

B. The victim should be confronted by someone other than the case agent, preferably the case agent's supervisor.

C. Use an empathetic approach.

D. Don't release information of the false allegation to the press.

BIBLIOGRAPHY

Burgess, Ann, R.N., Groth, Dr. Nicholas, Holmstrom, Lynda Lytle and Sgroi, Dr. Suzanne M, *Sexual Assault of Children and Adolescents*, Lexington Books

Forward, Susan and Buck, Craig, *Betrayal of Innocence*, Penquin Books

Rush, Florence, *Sexual Abuse of Children, The Best Kept Secret*, Prentice Hall

Tsang, Daniel, *Age Tabu, (The)*, Slyson Publications

American Psychiatric Association, Anonymous, *Incest Survivors "Open Letter to the Professional Community "and Nightmare of Incest*, Authored by Survivors, ISA, PO Box 5613, Long Beach, CA 90805-0613

Armstrong, Louise, *Kiss Daddy Goodnight*, Hawthorne Books Ind.

Baird, Elizabeth, *I was a Battered Child, Living Books, Tyndale House Publishers*

Brady, Katherine, *Father's Days*, Seaview Books

De Young, Mary, *Sexual Victimization of Children*, McFarland & Company.

Diagnostic and Statistical Manual of Mental Disorders, 3d Edition, Washington D.C.

Dziech, Billy Wright, and Schudson, Charles B, *On Trial-American Courts and their Treatment of Sexually Abused Children*, Beacon Press.

Eberle, Paul & Shirley, *Politics of Child Abuse (The)*, Secaucus/Lyle Stuart.

Finkelhor, David, *Sexually Victimized Children*, Free Press

Fox, Robin, *Red Lamp of Incest*, Dutton Publishers

Geiser, Robert, *Hidden Victims-The Sexual Abuse of Children*, Beacon Press

Gil, Elaina Dr., *Outgrowing The Pain*, Launch Press, Box 40174, San Francisco

Goldstein, Seth, *Sexual Exploitation of Children (The) -A Practical Guide to Assessment, Investigation, and Intervention*, Elsevier Service Publishing Co., Inc.

Groth, Nicholas, M.D., and Birnbaum, H. Jean, *Men Who Rape-the Psychology of the Offender*.

Groth, Nicholas, *Child Molester (The)*, Social Work and Child Sexual Abuse

Hayden, Torey L *One Child*, Avon Books, G.P. Putnam's Sons.

Herman, Judith Lewis, *Father-Daughter Incest*, Harvard Press

Hollingsworth, Jan, *Unspeakable Acts*, Congdon and Weed Publishers

BIBLIOGRAPHY

Irvine, Lucy, *Runaway,* Random House

Janus, Sam, *Death of Innocence (The),* Morrow Publishing Co.

Justice, Blair and Rita, *Abusing Family,(The),* Human Sciences Press

Justice, Blair and Rita, *Broken Taboo (The),* Human Sciences Press

Keys, Dr. Daniel, *Minds of Billy Mulligan (The),* Random House.

Lenderer, Laura, *Take Back the Night,* Everest House.

Meiselman, Dr. Karin Carlson, *Incest,* Jossey Bess Publishing

Miller, Alice, *Drama of the Gifted Child-The Search for the True Self,* Basic Books

Miller, Alice, *Thou Shalt Not Be Aware,* Basic Books

Morris, Michelle, *If I Should Die Before I Wake,* Tarc Publishers

Rogers, Dale Evans, Mead, Frank S, *Hear the Children Crying,* Power Books

Scriber, Flora Rheta, *Sybil,* Warner Books

Smith, Michelle, and Pazder, Lawrence, M.D., *Michelle Remembers,* Cogdon & Lottes, Inc.

Spencer, Judith, Suffer the Child, Pocket Books

Van Allen, Charlotte, Daddy's Girl, Simon & Schuster

Walterman, Jill and MacFarland, Kee, *Sexual Abuse of Young Children (The),* Guilford Press

Weisberg, Kelly, *Children of the Night,* Lexington Books.

Wolbert, Ann Burgess, *Child Pornography and Sex Rings,* Lextington Books.

Woodbury, John Ph D., *Silent Sin (The),* Elroy Schwartz. Signet Books

See Also:

The Accommodation Syndrome, A paper by Dr. Roland Summit. Published in the American Journal of Psychotherapy.

Dr. Gene Abel's published statistics on the *"Sexual Perpetrators-Their victims and their crimes."*. *Published by Johns Hopkins Hospital in American Medical Association Journals. (Available at most public libraries-research departments. or through Johns Hopkins Institute.)*

The National Center for Missing and Exploited Children (NCMEC) has published and make available several excellent **FREE** reference text books and pamphlets. Be sure to ask when you place your order if you'd like copies in another language; some of their publications are also available in Braille.

BIBLIOGRAPHY

Suggested readings:

- *Analysis: Interviewing Child Victims of Sexual Exploitation and Investigator's Guide.*
- *Children Traumatized in Sex Rings*
- *Child Molesters: A Behavioral Analysis*
- *Just in Case*

A series of informative brochures on prevention and intervention.

- *Missing and Abducted Children: A Law Enforcement Guide to Case Investigation.*
- *Sex Rings: A Behavioral Analysis of the Offender.*
- *Youth at Risk: (Runaways)*

Funded by the Office of Juvenile Delinquency and Planning, co-authored by the professionals at NCMEC, experienced FBI officers and other highly qualified individuals, these are "must have" materials for your library and may be obtained by writing to NCMEC, referencing the above titles and sending your request to:

The National Center for Missing & Exploited Children
2201 Wilson Boulevard, Suite 550
Arlington, VA 22201-3502.

If you want to call first and see if they have any "new releases" to add to your request, the phone number is 703-235-3900 or 1-800-The Lost.

INDEX

adult female perpetrator - adolescent male victim, 67
anti-logic, 143
ASAV: alleged sexual assault victim examination, 36
attention span, 21, 46
background information, 9, 53
background, 43
building rapport with a teen, 54
case selection, 119
clandestine telephone calls from victims, 69
cross-reporting to the child abuse registry, 38, 47
date rape / acquaintance rape, 69, 92
doing it correctly, 23
dolls, use of, 20
false reports, 31, 48, 70
family dynamics, 45
female anatomy, 114
female perpetrators - female victims, 65
female perpetrators - male victims, 65
first contact with the child using the stick figure system (SFS), 10
first contact with the victim, 53
five trademarks of a suspect interview, 132
get it right! get it all! get it the first time, 5
getting it all, 117
good touch vs. bad touch, 20
how did they become sex offenders?, 156
identifying body parts, 13
incest, 59
indicators of false allegations of sexual assault by strangers, 182
interview checklist, 42
interview of child 2-7 years using the stick figure system, 23
interview reports - confidentiality, 6
interview: 8-12 year-old victim, 48
interview: rape victim, 79
interviewing ages 13-18, 53
interviewing ages 18-80, 72
interviewing children ages 2-7, 8
interviewing children ages 8-12, 43
interviews at school, 38
male perpetrator - female victim, 59
male perpetrator - male victim, 57

INDEX

manipulation by victims, 54
medical exams, 70
mentally handicapped / retarded victims, 104
number of counts, 22, 45, 47
other victims, 23
out-of-home suspect, 44
photographs as evidence, 39
physical setting for the interview, 10
pre-drawn anatomy, 16
protective custody, 34
putting it all together, 159
qualifying as a witness, 20, 46
rape fantasy, 145
rape trauma syndrome, 179
rapport building, 12
repeating questions, 32
satanic cults, 107
seating arrangement, 43
secrets, 22
senile / elderly victims, 100
sex of interviewer, 70
something's not right, 149
spousal rape, 96
stranger rape, 70
tape-recording / videotaping, 32
teaming officers and advocates, 115
teaming with social services, 34, 44
terminology, 43
the five trademarks of a suspect interview, 132
time frames, 22
to tape or not to tape, 112
unlawful intercourse, 110
use of anatomically correct dolls, 20
victim / suspect profile, 44
victim gender, 45
when the suspect is a stranger, 72
when the victim wont talk, 113